PUBLIC ATTITUDES TOWARDS EDUCATION
IN ONTARIO 1996:
THE ELEVENTH OISE/UT SURVEY

D.W. LIVINGSTONE
D. HART
L.E. DAVIE

Public Attitudes towards Education in Ontario 1996

The Eleventh OISE/UT Survey

An OISE/UT book
published in association with
UNIVERSITY OF TORONTO PRESS
Toronto Buffalo London

© University of Toronto Press Incorporated 1997
Toronto Buffalo London
Printed in Canada

ISBN 0-8020-8039-1

∞

Printed on acid-free paper

Canadian Cataloguing in Publication Data

Main entry under title:

Public attitudes toward education in Ontario

(1980– : Informal series / Ontario Institute for Studies in Education)
Biennial.
1978–
"The OISE survey report."
Editors: D.W. Livingstone, D. Hart, and L.E. Davie
ISSN 1202-3558
ISBN 0-8020-8039-1 (1996)

1. Education – Ontario – Public opinion – Periodicals. 2. Public opinion – Ontario – Periodicals. I. Davie, Lynn. II. Hart, D.J., 1948– . III. Livingstone, D.W., 1943– . IV. Ontario Institute for Studies in Education. V. Title: Public attitudes towards education in Ontario. VI. Series: Informal series (Ontario Institute for Studies in Education).

LA418.O6P83   370'.9713   C95-390004-5

To contact authors, see details on pp. ix–x.

Cover photo: 'TVO Galaxy Classroom'

University of Toronto Press acknowledges the financial assistance to its publishing program of the Canada Council and the Ontario Arts Council.

Contents

PREFACE ix

Highlights 3

Introduction 9

Survey Design 11

1 General Views 13

　Views on the Province's Schools 13

　Views on Local Schools 16

2 Reorganizing Schooling 18

　School Careers, Common Curriculum, and Standards 19
　　School Careers: Early Childhood Education and Abolishing Grade 13 19
　　A Common Curriculum: Streaming and Compulsory Courses 21
　　Standards and Assessment 24

　Governing Schools 26
　　Public Influence and Parents' Councils 27
　　Influence over Curriculum 28
　　Increasing Public Influence: Mandates and Mechanisms 30
　　School Boards: Amalgamation or Oblivion 31
　　Control of Francophone Schools 33
　　Labour Relations 34

Equity   36
   Class Bias   37
   Girls- and Blacks-Only Schools   39
   Affirmative Action for Principalships   39
   Business Presence in the Schools   40

3 **Funding Schooling**   43

Public Funding for Education   43
   Budget Priorities   43
   Size of Expenditures   45
   Paying Education Taxes   49

Funding of Elementary and High Schools   51
   Redistribution of Education Taxes   51
   Property versus Income Taxes   51
   Funding for Catholic and Private Schools   53
   Fees for Junior Kindergarten   54
   Privatizing School Services   55

4 **Postsecondary Education**   57

Reorganization   58
   The Importance of Postsecondary Education   58
   Expansion and Differentiation   60
   Private Universities   62
   The College Sector and Sectoral Links: Findings from 1990, 1992, and 1994   64

Funding Choices   65
   Fee Hikes versus Cutbacks   65
   Cost Sharing by Government and Students   67
   Increases in Tuition Fees   68
   Differential Student Assistance   69
   Funding University Research   70

5 **Education and Work: Perceptions and Policies**   72

Perceptions   73
   Underused Skills   73
   Deserving a Better Job   74
   Enough Education?   75

    Causes of Unemployment   76
    Current Job Prospects   77
    Future Job Prospects   78
  Policies   78
    Workfare versus Training Strategies   79
    Canadian Research and Development   79
    Lower Wages or Shorter Workweeks?   80

6 Further Education, Computers, and Libraries   83

  Adult and Continuing Education   84

  Computers: Access and Impact   87
    Personal Access and Computer Skills   89
    Impact of Computerized Networks   91

  Roles for Libraries   93
    Access to Networks   93
    Importance for Adult Learners   94

APPENDIX: METHODS   99
  The Main Sample   99
    Sampling Procedures and Representativeness   99
    Changes in Methods fron Prior Surveys   100
    Categories of Background Variables   100
  The Supplementary Sample of Corporate Executives   103
  Sampling Tolerances   104

NOTES   107

Preface

We would like to acknowledge the wide variety of Ontario interest group representatives and individuals who have made suggestions to us over the past two years about relevant issues for the survey. We are grateful for the careful research assistance of Peter Sawchuk and for the expert word-processing skills of Christopher Richards. The survey is funded primarily through internal research grants from OISE. The Council of Ontario Universities and the Ministry of Culture and Communications have provided some supplementary funding for the present survey. While all this assistance has been very valuable, the authors remain solely responsible for the final design of items and for the interpretations of findings presented here.

We again invite comments and suggestions on this survey from all interested readers to:

OISE/UT Survey of Educational Issues
Ontario Institute for Studies in Education/University of Toronto
Department of Sociology in Education
252 Bloor Street West
Toronto, Ontario M5S 1V6

Attention: D.W. Livingstone

Direct inquiries may also be made to project staff:

by phone at (416) 923-6641: Livingstone (X2703); Hart (X2338); Davie (X2355);

or by FAX: (416) 926-4751;

or by e-mail:

dlivingston@oise.utoronto.on.ca
dhart@oise.utoronto.on.ca
ldavie@oise.utoronto.on.ca

PUBLIC ATTITUDES TOWARDS EDUCATION IN ONTARIO 1996:
THE ELEVENTH OISE/UT SURVEY

Highlights

General Views

- General satisfaction with Ontario's schools has increased over the first half of the 1990s. In 1988, only one-third of those surveyed were satisfied with the school system in general, compared to one-half in 1996. Satisfaction with local schools is somewhat higher (55 percent).
- Smaller proportions of the public are satisfied with value obtained for tax money in Ontario schools (40 percent) and with student discipline (30 percent).

Reorganizing Schooling

- A majority (56 percent) of the Ontario public support an earlier start to formal schooling by making early childhood (under age five) education available to all children whose parents choose to enrol them. In contrast, the public is about evenly divided over whether to shorten high school by abolishing Grade 13.
- There is growing public support for a common curriculum and a common school career for students throughout much of high school. Less than one-quarter of respondents would return to streaming students at grade 9 into distinct programs leading to university, college, or the workforce. There is now strong majority support for a core curriculum that includes English, mathematics, computer literacy, business or vocational studies, and science.
- Almost two-thirds favour higher standards for high school graduation even if this significantly reduces the number of graduates. A large majority (77 percent) think that students should have to pass

provincial examinations in all compulsory high school subjects in order to graduate.
- Two-thirds think that the public has too little say in how schools are run; about half of the public but two-thirds of parents would be willing to serve on a school council.
- The proportion of the public that want the provincial government to have the greatest influence over what is taught in local schools has dropped since the mid-1980s. Less than one-third now want the provincial (or federal) government to control curriculum; almost two-thirds favour local influences (school boards, teachers, or parents).
- Sixty percent favour merging school boards; smaller majorities support the more specific options of amalgamating public and Catholic, and English- and French-language boards. However, over two-thirds are opposed to getting rid of school boards altogether.
- A narrow majority (51 percent) support the right of francophones to control their own French-language schools. Views on this issue are unrelated to respondents' positions on merging English- and French-language boards.
- Support for teachers' right to strike has recently increased to 42 percent; however, a majority remain opposed. More respondents (46 percent) favour having school boards handle salary negotiations with teachers than want the provincial government (36 percent) to have this responsibility.
- Two-thirds think that children of low-income parents have less chance of getting a higher education than those of upper-income parents. Only one-third think that low-income parents place less value on their children's education than do upper-income parents.
- Large majorities are opposed to allowing school boards to establish separate high schools for girls (66 percent) or for black students (81 percent).
- Just under half (48 percent) support affirmative action to increase the proportion of elementary school principals who are women.

Funding Schooling

- A narrow majority give priority to maintaining health and educational services over deficit reduction or tax cuts. Deficit reduction is the priority of about one-quarter of the public, compared to less than 10 percent for tax cuts.

- Just under half (48 percent) favour a real (above inflation) increase in government spending for education; half are prepared to pay higher taxes in support of education.
- About four in five support the principle of transferring tax money from better-off to worse-off communities to equalize per-student spending across the province. The public is divided and increasingly uncertain, however, on one option for achieving this – replacing property taxes in support of education with an income tax.
- The public seems divided over what schools should receive public funding. Nearly 40 percent favour funding a unitary public system, one-third support the status quo of funding public and Catholic schools, while over one-quarter would extend funding to current private schools.
- The public is about evenly divided over whether parents should have to pay fees for junior kindergarten. A small majority (53 percent), however, support privatizing some school services such as busing.

Postsecondary Education

- About 70 percent of respondents rate getting a university or college education as very important; almost two-thirds now think that education beyond high school is needed to get along in present-day society.
- As has been the case since 1979, a majority (60 percent in the current survey) reject limiting enrolment in postsecondary programs based on availability of jobs for graduates. The public is about evenly divided over whether access to university education should be guaranteed for all students with the ability and interest, if this means spending more tax money on universities.
- Only small minorities favour reducing the number of universities (6 percent) or the number of programs offered at each university (17 percent).
- About 60 percent would allow private universities in Ontario; this figure is cut in half if private universities were to be allowed access to public funds for student assistance and research.
- The public is about equally divided over whether universities should respond to budget shortfalls mainly by raising fees, cutting programs, or reducing enrolments.
- The public appears prepared to see some increase in tuition fees to cover a higher proportion of the costs of a university education.

6 Public Attitudes towards Education in Ontario 1996

Nearly half would have government and students each bear half the cost; less than 20 percent want students to pay more than half. A small majority would allow universities to charge higher fees for professional programs where graduates are likely to earn higher incomes.
- About two-thirds recognize that higher fees would prevent students from low-income families from going to university. There is very widespread support (over 80 percent) for increasing financial assistance to students who have the ability and interest but lack the resources to go to university. A similar proportion favour income-contingent repayment of student loans.
- A majority (55 percent) favour increased funding for university research.

Education and Work: Perceptions and Policies

- Forty percent of employed respondents indicate that they have skills gained from experience and training that they would like to use at work but cannot.
- About one-third of employed respondents feel that they are entitled to a better job, based on their level of schooling.
- Thirty-five percent think that people have more education than their jobs require; 30 percent think that people generally have insufficient education for their work.
- Almost 60 percent think that the main cause of unemployment is that the economy is not generating enough jobs. Only one in five blames the schools for not preparing students for available jobs.
- A majority (55 percent) agree that there will not be enough jobs to go around no matter how much training and education people get.
- Sixty percent think that a university graduate is as likely to be unemployed as a high school graduate. Since 1982 a majority of the Ontario public have held this erroneous view. However, a large majority (84 percent) agree that a university graduate is more likely to obtain a better job, with a higher income, than a high school graduate.
- A large majority (69 percent) agree that Canada should spend more on research and development.
- A narrow majority (55 percent) would support a shorter standard workweek to increase employment; however, a large majority (66

percent) reject lowering the minimum wage for young people, even if this would create more jobs for youth.
- Only a minority (24 percent) think that workfare should be the focus of programs designed to get people off welfare and back to work; most respondents favour short-term (22 percent) or longer-term (39 percent) job training programs.

Further Education, Computers, and Libraries

- Twenty-eight percent of respondents report taking a continuing education course in the past year, down from over one-third in 1992. There was a significant increase in the number of courses taken at postsecondary institutions in 1996. Most course were taken at colleges (44 percent) or universities (27 percent). Most were credit courses.
- Over one-half of further education participants indicate that they took the courses to help them do their current jobs better (36 percent) or to prepare them for a new job (21 percent).
- Seventy percent paid for a course themselves; one-quarter took courses paid for by their employer. Most participants sought out their own courses; only one-quarter indicate that their employer, a government agency, or other organization either required or recommended the courses that they took.
- During the past year, respondents spent an average of almost twelve hours a week on informal learning activities related either to work or to their general interests. Unlike the case for participation in courses, the amount of time spent in informal learning is not higher among those with postsecondary education.
- Less than one-third (31 percent) report having no access to a personal computer at work or at home. Over half (56 percent) indicate that they have a home computer. Seventy percent of employed respondents report access to a personal computer at work.
- Almost two-thirds (62 percent) indicate that they can use a computer for functions such as word-processing and electronic mail.
- A large majority (70 percent) think that new computerized information networks will have a positive effect on people's lives.
- Two-thirds think that the government should be responsible for making sure that most people can connect to computer networks such as the Internet at an affordable cost.

- A majority think that public libraries would do a better job than others at providing public access to computerized networks (74 percent) and on-line government services (56 percent). A large majority (81 percent) think that public libraries should become the main access point to computerized networks for those who do not have access at home or at work.
- A large majority (77 percent) rate public libraries as very important to adult learners; 41 percent offer a similar rating for educational TV.
- Majorities rate public libraries as very important both for adults taking formal courses and for those engaged in learning activities on their own. Just under one-half think that public libraries are very important for those seeking information about local educational opportunities or information relevant to running a business.
- Most respondents (62 percent) support allowing public libraries to charge an annual membership fee.

Introduction

The government is clear about the need for a different education and training system ... This system is broken; neither parents nor the public are sure about which part of the education system is accountable for what.

John Snobolen, Ontario Minister of Education and Training[1]

Crisis has indeed gripped the educational community – a crisis of confidence. In the absence of vision, only guesswork and worry rule the landscape ... Parents, students, ratepayers and educators across Ontario are besieged by rumour and innuendo.

Chairpersons of Greater Toronto Area Public School Boards[2]

Public opinion can by definition only come into existence when a reasoning public is presupposed.

Jurgen Habermas[3]

In the past two years, there have probably been more structural changes proposed for Ontario's education system than during any comparable period in its history. In December 1994, after receiving thousands of deputations and written submissions, the Royal Commission on Learning made wide-ranging recommendations for the reorganization of virtually all aspects of elementary and secondary schooling.[4] Among the most substantial were expansion of kindergarten classes to three-year olds, the abolition of Grade 13, clearer guidelines for learning 'outcomes' within a common core curriculum, universal testing of students in Grades 3 and 11, standard report cards, a professional college of teachers, parents' councils at every school, and the equalization of per-pupil funding across the province. In the mid-1995 provincial election, the major parties all expressed agreement with the general direction proposed by the commission, and all vowed to reduce the amount of education spending outside the classroom.[5]

The new Progressive Conservative government rejected the expansion of kindergarten classes but has acted on other commission proposals, including abolishing Grade 13, introducing testing in Grades 3 and 11, standard report cards, a college of teachers, and local parents' councils, as well as developing more centrally determined core curricular guidelines.[6] As part of its overall plan to reduce deficit spending, the new government also made significant cuts to both school and postsecondary spending. These announced cuts led to an unprecedented series of mass protests against what demonstrators claimed was the destruction of public education.[7]

Throughout this period a series of other provincial commissions has made recommendations about more equitable ways of pooling education taxes, and provincial leaders have linked these proposals with the possible amalgamation or abolition of school boards.[8] After hearing many suggestions for reorganization of universities and community colleges, a provincial advisory panel on future directions for postsecondary education recommended greater specialization among institutions, deregulation of tuition fees, increased public funding, and permission to establish private universities.[9] Another report to the government recommended banning teachers' right to strike and defining extracurricular activities as part of their workday.[10] The issue of public funding for religious schools also remained prominent, with rejection of an appeal from Ontario Jewish and Christian schools by the Supreme Court and a successful constitutional initiative to end church domination of public schools in Newfoundland.[11] In September, 1996, Ontario's minister of education indicated that education reductions to date had been very modest, that bigger cuts were to come, and that Ontario was now 'looking at the biggest change in the structure of education in the province that's ever happened in my lifetime.'[12]

In periods of such substantial prospective change in education and other social policy areas, accurate readings of public opinion are essential to the process of genuinely democratic policy-making. Public opinion is the ultimate source of power in the liberal democratic state. Ideally, there are four basic stages in the formation of public opinion on any social issue: identification of policy options and summarizing the people's preliminary attitudes; wide dissemination of this information; extensive public deliberation on the options; and responsive decision making through authorized institutions.[13]

This process can be undermined in many ways. There is a persistent danger that those who control the major economic and political levers will dominate the identification and dissemination stages to serve their own interests, notably through distorted mass media portrayals of the issue, using leading questions in opinion polls, and either selectively reporting or suppressing poll results.[14] The deliberation and decision making stages can be monopolized by elite groups, even though their views may be no more consistent than those of the 'masses'[15] and mechanisms of more direct democratic policy making (such as electronic referenda and deliberative polling), are increasingly available and feasible.[16] In spite of these dangers, the general Canadian public retains views based on its own experience that are distinct from those expressed by political and economic elites, and there are strong indications in recent opinion polls that the vast majority want their governments to place more emphasis on consulting citizens.[17]

Though well-designed and widely disseminated opinion surveys on policy issues provide no guarantee of responsive policy decisions, they are necessary first steps in large, modern societies. The basic purpose of the biennial OISE/UT Survey of Educational Issues in Ontario is to provide regular representative readings of the public's views on pertinent policy issues, so as to enhance the general public's collective self-awareness and increase informed participation in the making of educational policy. The 1996 OISE/UT Survey is the eleventh in a series that began in 1978.[18] It remains the only regular, publicly disseminated survey of public attitudes towards educational policy options in Canada.[19] It offers both trend data and current profiles of public support for existing educational programs and proposed policy changes in Ontario. In the context of the wide array of currently proposed structural changes, the 1996 survey should be especially relevant to present public deliberation and policy decisions in education.

Survey Design

The 1996 OISE/UT survey involves a representative random sample of 1,000 adults, eighteen years of age and older, who were interviewed via telephone in their residences across Ontario between September 30 and November 3, 1996. The survey was administered by the Institute for Social Research at York University and achieved a response rate of 63 percent. The face-to-face interviewing procedure used in the OISE/UT surveys up to 1992 is no longer feasible, but we are confident that the telephone technique used in 1994 and 1996 has not decreased the representativeness of our sample. As in all prior studies, a supplementary sample of corporate executives (114 respondents) also replied to a mailed questionnaire during the same period. The Appendix contains a discussion of the changed sampling and interviewing methods, a description of the sample composition, and guidelines for interpreting statistical differences. Most tables present the wording of questions; the full questionnaire is available from the authors on request.

In reporting our 1996 results, we refer whenever possible to comparable items from the previous OISE/UT surveys as well as from other relevant surveys. Much of the distinctive value of the OISE/UT survey stems from the capacity that it offers readers to track opinion trends on an increasing number of issues by periodically repeating the same questions. Responses to each question have been analysed in relation to various social background variables. These include: age, sex, contact with schools, schooling, religion, mother tongue, ethnicity, family income, occupational class, and geographical region. Only current statistically significant differences on these factors are reported in the text and usually displayed in the tables. The reported findings should not be generalized to specific localities.

1
General Views

In this first chapter we look at how satisfied or dissatisfied the Ontario public is with schools in the province, and with the schools in their own community. In each case we present findings regarding satisfaction with:

- the school system in general
- value obtained for taxpayers' money
- student discipline

Views on the Province's Schools

Each OISE/UT survey questionnaire has typically begun by asking respondents for their general views about the school system. Over the years we have tracked both respondents' perceptions of whether the quality of education has improved or deteriorated and their satisfaction or dissatisfaction with the current situation in Ontario's schools. Responses are a barometer of the public's overall sentiments about the school system; they provide an indication of how much urgency the public may attach to educational reform (though not the direction that reform should take).

Within broad limits, it is the trend in public views rather than the actual level of satisfaction or dissatisfaction that yields the more valuable information. How questions are worded and where they are placed in an interview schedule can have a strong influence on how people respond. Thus comparing specific levels of satisfaction across surveys can be like comparing apples and oranges if those surveyed were asked different questions. In the case of the OISE/UT survey we meet this problem by asking questions with the same wording and in about the same position in the interview from year to year. The format of the questions on satisfaction, by including a middle option 'neither agree nor disagree' (in addition to accepting 'don't knows') probably discourages those with weakly held opinions from choosing an 'agree' or 'disagree' option. As a result, the survey typically records lower proportions of satisfied (and dissatisfied) respondents than do polls using questions without a middle option. Both formats are equally acceptable; problems arise when comparisons are made across polls without reference to the questions asked.[20]

In 1994, we focused on the public's views on what had happened to the quality of education over the previous five years. The results indicated that opinions about the direction of change in the high schools had probably been stable for at least a decade. Views on changes in quality in elementary schools in 1994 were similar to what they had been in 1984. At both levels, more respondents thought quality had deteriorated than thought it had improved. There was, however, no indication of a sharp increase in the proportion who saw a decline; in other words, there was no indication that the public saw the schools as having reached a 'crisis point' with regard to the quality of education.

In 1996 we ask respondents about their satisfaction or dissatisfaction with the school system in general, repeating a question first asked in 1979 and last asked in the 1990 OISE/UT survey. We also repeat two questions not asked since 1982, about satisfaction with value received for taxpayers' money and satisfaction with student discipline. The results are shown in **Table 1.1**.

Satisfaction with the school system has fluctuated more widely over time than have perceptions of changes in the quality of education. As shown in **Table 1.1**, the proportion of the public who indicated that they are satisfied with the school system declined from over one-half in 1982 to just over one-third in 1988. Positive opinion of the school system recovered, however, in the late 1980s and the first half of the 1990s. In 1996, half of respondents indicate that they are satisfied with the school system in general; about one-third are dissatisfied. If there was a 'crisis point' in public satisfaction with the schools, it was likely in the late 1980s, when public opinion was almost equally divided, rather than the current decade.

As for public satisfaction with value obtained for taxes and with student discipline, we cannot track opinion over the 1980s and early 1990s. The pattern of public opinion in 1996 is virtually identical to

TABLE 1.1 How satisfied are you with the current situation in Ontario elementary and high schools with regard to …?

	Satisfied %	Dissatisfied %	Neither/ not stated %	N
The school system in general				
1979	50	30	20	1084
1980	51	29	20	1050
1982	55	24	21	1050
1986	42	33	25	1042
1988	36	37	28	1011
1990	47	29	25	1032
1996	50	34	16	1000
Value obtained for taxpayers' money				
1980	40	40	20	1108
1982	40	39	21	1050
1996	40	39	21	1000
Student discipline				
1980	33	52	15	1108
1982	32	49	19	1150
1996	30	53	18	1000

what we found in 1980 and in 1982 (see **Table 1.1**). If there was, in fact, a decline in satisfaction on these issues in the mid-1980s, there must also have been recovery. In all years for which we have complete data, satisfaction with value for taxes and satisfaction with discipline are less common than satisfaction with the school system in general. Opinion is about equally divided on value obtained for tax monies; in 1980, 1982, and 1996 about half of respondents indicate that they are dissatisfied with student discipline.

Satisfaction with schools decreases with age. Just over a third of respondents over sixty-five report that they are satisfied with the school system in general, compared to two-thirds of those under twenty-five (see **Table 1.2**). We find similar age differences in satisfaction with value obtained and with student discipline. Parents are somewhat more likely than non-parents to be satisfied with value obtained (47 versus 37 percent) and with student discipline (41 versus 25 percent). Differences are, however, greater in views on local schools (see below).

Views held by corporate executives are considerably more negative than those of the general public. Fifty-nine percent are dissatisfied with

16   Public Attitudes towards Education in Ontario 1996

TABLE 1.2 How satisfied are you with the current situation in Ontario elementary and high schools with regard to the school system in general?

	Satisfied %	Dissatisfied %	Neither/ not stated %	N
Age				
18-24	67	23	11	133
25-34	53	29	18	236
35-44	52	35	13	208
45-54	45	41	15	143
55-64	46	39	15	118
65+	35	42	23	143

the school system in general; 72 percent, with value obtained for taxes, and 69 percent, with student discipline.

Views on Local Schools

A consistent finding of the U.S. Gallup Poll of attitudes towards schools has been that respondents offer more positive views of local schools than they do of the nation's schools.[21] In 1996, for the first time, we asked respondents about their satisfaction with schools in their own community as well as with Ontario schools in general. As **Table 1.3**

TABLE 1.3 How satisfied are you with the current situation in elementary and high schools in your community with regard to ...?

	Satisfied %	Dissatisfied %	Neither/ not stated %	N
School system in general	54	23	23	1000
Value for taxpayers' money	46	33	21	1000
Student discipline	35	46	20	1000

indicates, they are somewhat more likely to report satisfaction with their local school than with schools in the province as a whole. This is the case whether the question deals with the school system in general, value for taxpayers' money, or student discipline. These differences are, however, much smaller than have been found in the U.S. Gallup Poll, which asks respondents to assign a letter grade to schools rather than indicate whether or not they are satisfied with the school system.

Differences in satisfaction between parents and non-parents are, however, greater for community schools than for provincial schools. Over 60 percent of parents are satisfied with their local system, compared to just under one-half of non-parents. Almost one-half of parents are satisfied with student discipline, compared to less than one-third of non-parents. Differences between parents and non-parents reflect both the more positive views of parents and the higher proportions of non-parents who do not offer a definite opinion.

2
Reorganizing Schooling

In this chapter we present public views on a wide range of issues concerning the reorganization of elementary and secondary education in Ontario. The chapter is divided into three main sections. The first deals with school careers, curriculum, and standards, including the following issues:

- access to early childhood education
- abolishing Grade 13
- destreaming Grade 9
- compulsory high school subjects
- higher standards for high school graduation
- provincial examinations at high school

The second section covers issues concerning school governance and labour relations, including:

- public say on how schools are run
- personal willingness to serve on a school council
- who should have the greatest influence over curriculum
- merging school boards
- getting rid of school boards
- control of French-language schools
- teachers' right to strike
- local versus province-wide bargaining

The third section deals with a number of issues of equity, including:

- educational opportunities of children of low and upper income parents
- value placed on education by low and upper income parents
- separate high schools for girls
- separate high schools for blacks
- affirmative action in appointing principals
- presenting the business perspective in schools
- allowing advertising in schools

School Careers, Common Curriculum, and Standards

As the eleventh OISE/UT survey was being conducted, parents across Ontario had just encountered another questionnaire – this one from the Ontario Ministry of Education and Training. In late September 1996 the ministry released a discussion paper on reorganizing high school education. *Excellence in Education: High School Reform*[22] covered both areas where policy decisions had already been announced – notably, abolishing Grade 13 – and new proposals, including a new organization of compulsory courses and streamed courses on which readers were invited to provide advice. Included with the discussion paper was a questionnaire inviting parental views in four areas: destreaming or restreaming Grade 9, formats for extending the number of compulsory courses, work experience and cooperative education programs and province-wide standards and testing. The current survey provides an indication of the public's predispositions in three of these areas – destreaming, compulsory courses, and provincial testing – as well as on abolishing Grade 13. Our prior surveys have found strong support for cooperative education.

School Careers: Early Childhood Education and Abolishing Grade 13

As noted above, the Royal Commission on Learning recommended reshaping schooling at both ends, by making early childhood education universally available for three-year-olds while at the same time abolishing Grade 13. The current government has rejected the recommendations for universal, voluntary early childhood education, made junior kindergarten optional, and cut financial support at the same time. It has indicated that Grade 13 will be eliminated, though this change has now been delayed so that the first student cohort will

TABLE 2.1
Views on early childhood education and abolishing Grade 13

	Agree %	Disagree %	Don't know %	N
Education programs should be available in all Ontario school boards to all children 3–5 years of age whose parents choose to enrol them.	56	36	8	1000
Grade 13 should be abolished in Ontario high schools.	42	46	12	1000

graduate from the new four-year high school program in 2002. Current government policy thus entails shortening school careers overall rather than altering the time frame in order to shift resources to education at younger ages, as the royal commission proposed. The eleventh OISE/UT survey asked respondents about their views both on universal early childhood education and on abolishing Grade 13.

A majority of the Ontario public support making early childhood education available across the province to all children aged three to five whose parents choose to enrol them. In contrast, the public is about evenly divided over whether or not to abolish Grade 13 (see **Table 2.1**).

Almost 60 percent of respondents support making early childhood education (ECE) universally available. Parents and non-parents hold similar views on this issue. However, views are strongly related to age (see **Table 2.2**). Over three-quarters of those under twenty-five support extending ECE. In contrast, those age forty-five and older are divided, with a narrow majority opposed. Those who report non-European ethnicity are more likely to favour ECE than those who identify their ethnic group as British. A majority of corporate executives (62 percent) oppose making ECE universally available.

Ontarians are divided on the question of abolishing Grade 13; 42 percent agree while 46 disagree with the policy. Even among corporate executives who consistently support restriction of educational services (or oppose the extension of services), there is uncertainty. A narrow majority of executives (54 percent) support abolishing Grade 13, but one in five is opposed, and one-quarter are unwilling or unable to offer an opinion. Parents of elementary school students hold views similar to those of the general population. A majority (56 percent) of

TABLE 2.2
'Education programs should be available in all Ontario school boards to all children 3-5 years of age whose parents choose to enrol them.'

	Agree %	Disagree %	Don't know %	N
All respondents	56	36	8	1000
Age				
18-24	78	16	7	133
25-34	66	23	11	236
35-44	55	36	9	208
45-54	47	50	4	143
55-64	43	53	4	118
65+	43	50	7	143
Ethnic group				
British	50	44	6	498
French	52	42	6	76
Other European	61	31	8	227
Non-European	72	17	11	77

parents of high school students oppose the policy.[23] While the views of these parents appear distinct, sampling error (the luck of the draw in selecting our sample) could account for most of this difference.

A Common Curriculum: Streaming and Compulsory Courses

Excellence in Education: High School Reform reopens the issue of de-streaming Grade 9, instituted by the previous government in 1993. Parents are asked which of two options they prefer. Under the first option Grade 9 students take a common curriculum without being separated into classes according to whether they plan to go to university or college or enter the workforce after high school. Under the second option students are streamed, taking courses designed for their different destinations. The discussion paper also asks for parents' views on compulsory courses. In this case, parents are asked to evaluate nine options with varying weights of compulsory versus optional courses and particular subject concentrations. The options assume that the same subjects (though not specific courses) would be compulsory for all students, regardless of whether they planned to continue their education after high school or enter the labour force.

The OISE/UT surveys have tracked public opinion on streaming since 1980. In addition, the 1996 survey repeated a question on compulsory

TABLE 2.3
'At which grade, if at all, should the schools stream or separate students into different programs intended to prepare some students directly for the world of work and other students for entry into community college or university?'

	Not at all %	Grade 12 or 13 %	Grade 11 %	Grade 10 %	Grade 9 or earlier %	Don't know/ not stated %	N
All respondents							
1980	5	12	18	21	39	5	1108
1982	7	19	16	17	36	5	1050
1988	10	16	17	20	30	8	1011
1990	13	15	15	20	32	5	1032
1992	21	20	18	14	25	2	1000
1994	13	13	14	19	32	9	1070
1996	15	25	17	16	21	6	1000

courses not asked since 1984. Respondents were invited to indicate what subjects they would make compulsory for high school students, depending on their goals after leaving high school: university or a full-time job. This question allows us to assess views both on the extent to which the high school curriculum should be made up of compulsory subjects and the extent to which these subjects should be the same for all students regardless of their plans.

In 1996 the results of both questions indicate strong public support for a common curriculum and a common school career throughout much of high school. As **Table 2.3** indicates, support for streaming at Grade 9, after a brief resurgence in 1994, has again declined. Less than one-quarter of respondents support a return to streaming at the beginning of high school; 40 percent would either abolish streaming altogether or stream only in the final year of high school. Attitudes on this issue are similar across social groups. In particular, parents and non-parents hold similar opinions. While there is overwhelming public support for destreaming, a survey conducted by the Ontario Secondary School Teachers' Federation (OSSTF) indicates that teachers are not convinced that it benefits their students.[24]

Excellence in Education: High School Reform envisions an increase in the weight of compulsory courses within the high school curriculum (and invites public views on a limited range of models). A comparison of findings from the 1984 and 1996 OISE/UT surveys suggests that this proposal is in line with a shift in public views on compulsory subjects.

TABLE 2.4
'If you were the one making the decision, would you require every high school student planning to attend university/planning to get a full time job after high school to take: ...?'*

	Planning to attend university		Planning to get a full time job	
	1984 % yes	1996 % yes	1984 % yes	1996 % yes
Mathematics	80	96	65	96
Use of computers	57	95	54	96
English†	54	98	43	97
Science	46	84	21	68
Business or vocational studies	36	75	69	88
French	35	49	27	48
History	33	63	15	45
Art and music	11	29	6	19
	N=1046	N=1000	N=1046	N=1000

* In 1984 the list of subjects included geography, social sciences, and physical and health education.
† In 1984, this option was 'language of instruction in the school (English or French).'

Public opinion surveys have provided comparatively little information about public attitudes towards compulsory courses and how they may have changed over time. In 1984, our sixth survey asked respondents which of a list of subjects they would make compulsory for high school students intending to go to university, for those planning on attending community college, and for students hoping for full-time employment. The results indicated that Ontarians were, in general, reluctant to make subjects compulsory at high school. There was majority support for making only three subjects compulsory for university-bound students: mathematics, computer literacy, and English; for students headed for the workforce, a majority again favoured making mathematics and computer literacy mandatory but substituted vocational and business studies for English.

In 1996 we revisit the issue of compulsory courses using an abbreviated version of the question asked in 1984. (Fewer subjects are listed; we ask only about students bound for university or the job market.) As **Table 2.4** indicates, there has been a sharp increase in support for making subjects compulsory in high school. Large majorities of respondents favour making six of eight subjects listed mandatory for students planning to attend university. As in 1984, support is highest for mathematics, computer literacy, and English; in

1996 there is virtual unanimity that these subjects should be required. Science, business and vocational studies, and history now also receive majority support; almost half of respondents would also make French compulsory.

Those surveyed make little distinction in their choices of compulsory subjects according to students' plans for the future. In the case of students intending to seek employment after high school, respondents are again virtually unanimous in favouring compulsory courses in mathematics, computer literacy, and English. Compulsory business or vocational studies also receive a very high level of support; a smaller majority favour making science a required subject. Just under one-half want history and French as compulsory subjects.

These results suggest that the Ontario public has moved towards a stronger consensus on what should constitute a common curriculum for high school. At the core are old and new basics on which virtually everyone is agreed: English, mathematics, and computer literacy. Science and business/vocational studies are included by most respondents. Near-majorities also would include history and French, regardless of destination after high school. (The list of subjects offered to respondents was not inclusive.)

Views on compulsory courses are similar across social groups, except that support for requiring history, particularly for students planning to enter the job market, increases with age. Only 26 percent of respondents under twenty-five would make history compulsory for these students compared to 53 percent of those over sixty-five. Corporate executives differ from the general population in distinguishing among required subjects according to the destination of students. Only a minority (38 percent) would make business or vocational studies compulsory for students bound for university or require science (33 percent) for those planning to enter the workforce.

Standards and Assessment

Excellence in Education: High School Reform embraces the idea of higher standards and asks for parents' views on province-wide testing. Calls for higher standards almost always take it for granted that these would be well within the reach of most students. In 1996, the OISE/UT survey followed the lead of the U.S. Gallup poll in asking respondents whether they would favour higher standards if it meant that significantly fewer students would graduate. The Ontario discussion

TABLE 2.5
'Would you favour setting higher standards for students graduating from high school, even if this meant that significantly fewer students would graduate than is now the case?'

	%
Yes	64
No	25
Not sure	11

N=1000

paper asks parents what subjects at what grades should be tested across the province. The OISE/UT survey asked respondents about one key option: reinstituting province-wide examinations for all compulsory subjects.

As shown in **Table 2.5**, almost two-thirds of Ontario respondents want higher standards for high school graduation, even if significantly fewer students graduate. This pattern is virtually identical to that found in 1995 by the U.S. Gallup poll.[25] Support for higher standards is general across social groups. Majority support for higher standards does not imply that most people think that the quality of high school education has eroded. Perceptions of change in the quality of education have held largely stable for at least a decade.[26]

Past OISE/UT surveys have documented growing majority support for using province-wide tests to assess each elementary and secondary student. By 1992, almost three-quarters favoured province-wide testing at the elementary level; in 1994 we recorded a similar level of support for such testing in high schools. While there can be little doubt that the public supports province-wide testing, it is much less obvious what testing is to be for. (The questionnaire included with *Excellence in Education* asks parents precisely this.) In particular, it is unclear to what extent the public wants tests to determine individual students' progress through the system. In 1994, we found respondents about equally divided on the issue of whether final grades should reflect mainly teachers' assessments or the results of province-wide tests.[27] *Excellence in Education* contemplates the possibility of reintroducing compulsory exit examinations for high school students. The Ontario Council of Parents' response to the discussion paper voices support for an exit exam in literacy as a short-term policy and exit examinations, worth up to 50 percent of final marks, for all Grade 12 or Ontario Academic Credit (OAC) subjects in the longer term.[28]

TABLE 2.6
'Students should have to pass a provincial examination in each compulsory subject in order to graduate from high school?'

	%
Agree	77
Disagree	18
Neither/not stated	5

N=1000

The 1996 OISE/UT survey includes a new question on testing which reflects the long-term policy position of the Ontario Council of Parents. Respondents were asked whether high school students should have to pass a provincial examination in each compulsory subject in order to graduate. (Respondents encountered this question after they had indicated what subjects they would make compulsory. There were several intervening questions before the item on testing.) As **Table 2.6** indicates, a large majority of respondents agree with instituting provincial examinations in compulsory subjects. Support for provincial exams is general across social groups; corporate executives are distinct only by being almost unanimous on this issue.

Taken together, public views on compulsory courses and on provincial examinations in compulsory subjects amount to strong support for a relatively broad common curriculum with provincially enforced standards. Is this also a mandate for centralization of control over elementary and secondary schooling? We take up this issue in the next section.

Governing Schools

Among the most volatile issues in education are those concerning governance. At the time of the 1994 OISE/UT survey, the most prominent issue was school-parent councils and the extent to which authority over what happened in local schools would be delegated to local communities. Amalgamation of school boards was also much discussed. In 1996, while parent councils are still 'with us,' the big issue is the fate of school boards, and more specifically the extent to which decision-making about spending levels and curriculum should be centralized in the provincial government. Amalgamation has now been recommended by the final report of the Ontario School Board Reduction Task Force (Sweeney Report)[29] established by the

TABLE 2.7
'How do you feel about the amount of say the general public has in how schools are run?'

	Too much say %	Enough say %	Too little say %	Don't know/ not stated %	N
1979*	6	41	49	5	758
1984*	6	32	53	10	753
1990	6	29	60	5	1032
1994	5	25	64	6	1070
1996	7	23	64	6	1000

* From 1979 and 1984 polls by Canadian Education Association (CEA) of Canadian opinion on education: CEA Task Force on Public Involvement in Educational Decisions, *Results of a Gallup Poll of Public Opinion in Canada about Public Involvement in Educational Decisions* (Toronto: CEA, 1979); G.E. Flower *Speaking Out: The 1984 CEA Poll of Canadian Opinion on Education* (Toronto: CEA, 1984).

former NDP government; public discussions have broadened further to include the possibility of eliminating the boards altogether. On January 13, 1997, the minister announced that school boards would be retained but would be reduced in number.

Labour relations in the school sector have also become highly controversial in the past year. A government-commissioned report recommends that the current right of teachers to strike be removed.[30] The government has also signalled an interest in moving to province-wide bargaining, supplanting the current system, where school boards negotiate contracts with the teachers' federations.

Public Influence and Parents' Councils

How involved or how excluded does the public feel in the running of schools? In 1996, almost two-thirds of respondents indicate that the general public had too little say in how schools are run, unchanged since 1994 (see **Table 2.7**). Perceptions that public influence on schools is not adequate have grown significantly since 1979, when just under one-half of Ontario respondents to a survey sponsored by the Canadian Education Association (CEA) indicated that the public had too little say. Views are similar across social groups.

More than general sentiments about public influence have changed since the early 1980s. There has been a parallel increase in willingness to become personally involved in school governance. The CEA's 1979

TABLE 2.8
'If asked today, would you or would you not serve on a local school parent council?'

	1994 %	1996 %
Definitely	17	18
Probably	32	34
Probably not	28	23
Definitely not	22	21
Not stated	2	3

N=1000

survey found only one-third of Ontario respondents willing to serve on school advisory committees or home and school committees.[31] In both 1994 and 1996, about half of respondents indicate that they would 'probably' or 'definitely' be willing to do so (see **Table 2.8**). Two-thirds of parents of children in elementary and/or high school indicate that they would probably or definitely be willing to serve, compared to just under one-half of those with no children in school. Willingness to become involved is also related to age and the respondent's own schooling. Less than half of those over fifty-five indicate that they would participate, compared to majorities of younger age groups. Sixty percent of respondents with postsecondary education would serve, compared to about four in ten with less formal education. Willingness to serve is not related to overall views as to whether the general public had sufficient influence on how schools are run.

Influence over Curriculum

In 1994 we explored public views on how much responsibility should be delegated to school councils in regard to school programs. In 1996, we examine curriculum control more broadly, offering respondents a range of centralized and decentralized options. An issue common to both years is the role of school boards.

In 1994 there was both widespread enthusiasm for establishing school councils and general wariness about entrusting them with too much responsibility. The Ontario Parent Council, while making a strong appeal for increasing parental influence, proposed only an advisory role in key school policy areas such as curriculum, budgeting, and staffing for the local school councils that it recommended.[32] The Royal Commission on Learning's recommendation on school councils had more to do with making community resources available to the

TABLE 2.9
'In your opinion, who should have the greatest influence in deciding what is taught in the schools in your community?'

	1984 %	1996 %
The federal government	15	10
The provincial government	31	19
Local school boards	21	23
Local teachers	9	13
Parents of school children	18	29
Can't say	5	6

N=1000

schools than with exerting parental or community influence on school policies.[33] The 1994 OISE/UT survey asked respondents whether boards or school parent councils should have the main responsibility in a number of policy areas. In most policy areas, about one-half of respondents favoured leaving that role with school boards. Up to one-quarter favoured boards and councils' sharing responsibility. As for making decisions about school programs, 53 percent wanted boards to be mainly responsible; one-quarter favoured a joint system, while only about one in five wanted school parents' councils to have the main responsibility.[34]

In 1996, we asked who should have the greatest influence in deciding what is taught in local schools, with the options shown in **Table 2.9**. This question had originally been asked in the fifth OISE/UT survey in 1984. Comparing results for the two surveys, more than a decade apart, we find that the proportion of respondents who select school boards is virtually identical: 21 percent in 1984, 23 percent in 1996. What has changed is the level of public support for centralizing control over curriculum. In 1984, almost half of respondents favoured either the provincial or the federal government's having the greatest influence; in 1996, both these options lose ground, attracting the combined support of less than one-third of respondents. In 1996, there is somewhat more support for local teachers' having the most influence; the greatest change, however, is in support for according parents this role. In 1996, this option is the most frequently cited by respondents, having increased from 18 to 29 percent.

Views on who should have the most influence on the curriculum in local schools are similar across social groups particularly between parents and non-parents. Corporate executives, however, are much more likely than the general public to favour the provincial government's having the greatest say over curriculum; in 1996, 47 percent hold this view. Even for this group, however, support for centralizing options is lower than in 1984, when 56 percent wanted the province to have the most influence.

Increasing Public Influence: Mandates and Mechanisms

There are a number of ways to read public views on influence over curriculum. From one perspective, the 1996 results indicate a decline in confidence in government bodies. A bare majority now opt for having established agencies, mainly the provincial government or school boards, retain the greatest influence over local curriculum, compared to two-thirds in 1984. From another perspective, the results indicate a decline specifically in support for centralizing control over local curriculum; support for local boards' control is undiminished. This interpretation is consistent with our finding that the public is resistant to abolishing school boards and transferring their responsibilities to the provincial government, as outlined below.

If resistance to centralization is an important message in the results, what does this mean for school boards? In 1996, almost twice as many respondents wanted parents or local teachers to have the greatest influence on local curriculum as favoured school boards. Thus among respondents who favour local options (that is, oppose centralization to the provincial government or beyond), almost two in three apparently want a greater voice for a vehicle representing the views of parents and teachers, below the level of school boards. A version of school councils (notably the Alberta model[35]) appears tailor-made for this role. Yet our 1994 findings indicated that only a minority of the public were currently willing to transfer responsibility for curriculum from school boards to school councils.

Currently, opinion leaders' debate over control of local school curriculum concerns the balance of power between school boards and the provincial Ministry of Education and Training. For the general public, however, the issue is drawn differently. The 1996 OISE/UT survey suggests a three-way divide among a shrinking proportion of the public who favour centralization, a stable proportion for whom local school boards are appropriate, and a growing number who favour more say for teachers and parents.

Above we reported very widespread support for requiring high school students to meet more exacting standards in order to graduate and for enforcing standards through province-wide examinations. Among educators, such standards and examinations imply centralization of real control over curriculum through a host of pressures on teachers to 'teach to the test.' This is an assumption that is not shared by the general public. Supporters and opponents of centralization hold similar views on raising standards and on testing. In other words, neither support for provincial examinations nor a desire for higher graduation standards implies support for centralizing responsibility for the school system with the provincial government.

School Boards: Amalgamation or Oblivion

Amalgamation of school boards has been embraced by both NDP and Conservative governments as a policy for rechannelling resources from school board administration to the classroom. It has been opposed by the boards themselves, by proponents of local control of schooling, and by those who question the purported savings. Amalgamation raises issues beyond administrative boundaries when it involves joining public and Catholic boards or merging English- and French-language boards. In 1996, the minister of education and training indicated that eliminating school boards altogether, as had been done in New Brunswick,[36] was under consideration.

The 1996 OISE/UT survey indicates there is a broad consensus among Ontarians both that the number of school boards should be reduced through amalgamation, and that school boards should continue to exist.

In both 1994 and 1996, about 60 percent of respondents to the OISE/UT survey agreed that Ontario should have fewer school boards, each covering more schools (see **Table 2.10**). In 1996, over one-half favour merging public and Catholic boards and French and English boards (see **Table 2.11**). The strongest resistance to amalgamation comes from those under twenty-five (see **Table 2.10**). Within this group, opinion is about evenly divided over amalgamation in general and over more specific proposals to merge public and Catholic boards, and French and English boards. Non-parents and those with children in public school hold similar views. However, a majority (51 percent) of those with children in the Catholic system reject

TABLE 2.10
'Ontario should have fewer school boards, each covering a larger number of schools.'

	Agree %	Disagree %	Neither/ not stated %	N
All respondents				
1994	58	28	14	1070
1996	60	28	12	1000
Age				
18–24	42	36	23	133
25–34	56	23	21	236
35–44	56	25	19	208
45–54	63	20	17	143
55–64	68	16	16	118
65+	57	27	16	143

TABLE 2.11
'Do you support or oppose, and how strongly, each of the following types of school board mergers?'

	Favour %	Oppose %	Neither/ not stated %	N
Merging public and Catholic boards	55	28	17	1000
Merging French and English boards	57	24	19	1000

amalgamating public and separate boards. It was not possible to identify parents of children in schools operated by French-language boards. Majorities of those who report their first language as French or their ethnic origin as French support amalgamation of French- and English-language boards. However, as is discussed below, support for merging English- and French-language boards is not seen by respondents as precluding the right of francophones to manage their own schools. Finally, corporate executives are even more supportive (87 percent) of amalgamating school boards than the general public.

Support for amalgamating boards is highest among those who favour centralizing control of curriculum (see **Table 2.10**), and lowest among those who want school boards to have the greatest influence on what is taught locally. However, a substantial majority of respondents who want teachers or parents to have the most influence also support amalgamation of boards.

TABLE 2.12
'Do you support or oppose, and how strongly, getting rid of school boards altogether, with the provincial government taking over decisions on curriculum and spending?'

	%
Support	22
Oppose	69
Neither/not stated	9

N=1000

Immediately after providing their views on amalgamation, respondents were asked whether they agreed or disagreed with getting rid of school boards altogether, with the provincial government taking over decisions on curriculum and spending. As shown in **Table 2.12**, over two-thirds disagree with getting rid of boards and centralizing their responsibilities with the provincial government. Parents and non-parents hold similar views on this issue. Older respondents are more willing to consider eliminating boards; however, even among those sixty-five and older, one-half are opposed. Resistance to getting rid of school boards is highest (85 percent) among those who indicate that they want boards to have the greatest say in local curriculum; however, even among those who favour centralized control, a narrow majority oppose eliminating boards. In contrast to the general public, a majority (54 percent) of corporate executives favour getting rid of school boards altogether.

Control of Francophone Schools

A majority of the public, even those who identify their first language or ethnic origin as French, support amalgamation of French and English school boards. The 1996 survey also repeated a question from 1994 asking whether Ontario's francophones should control their own French-language schools. In 1994, respondents had been almost equally divided, and in 1996, a narrow majority support francophone rights (see **Table 2.13**). Clear majorities of those who indicate that their first language is French (67 percent) or who report their ethnic origin as French (63 percent) support francophone control of schools, compared to about one-half of other groups. Older respondents are less supportive than those in younger age groups; less than one-half of respondents fifty-five to sixty-four, and only one-quarter of those sixty-five and older agree with francophone rights in this area.

TABLE 2.13
'Ontario francophones should have the right to control and manage their own French-language school anywhere in the province where there are enough students.'

	1994 %	1996 %
Agree	46	51
Disagree	48	40
Neither/not stated	6	9

N=1070

There is no relationship between views on this issue and support or resistance to amalgamating English- and French-language boards. Those who support amalgamation are as likely to favour francophone control of schools as those who are opposed to merging French and English boards.

Labour Relations

In August 1996 the provincial government began a review of Bill 100, for the past two decades the legal basis for collective bargaining between teachers and school boards. The report of that review, issued in November 1996,[37] recommended, among other changes, ending teachers' legal right to strike, making after-hours extra-curricular activities part of normal workload (hence weakening 'work to rule' job actions), and more centralized collective bargaining, with negotiations conducted by regional groupings of boards rather than individual boards.

The OISE/UT surveys have been tracking public opinion on teachers' right to strike since 1980. As **Table 2.14** indicates, public views, largely stable over the past decade and a half, shifted significantly from 1994 to 1996 towards greater support for the right to strike, though a majority would still deny teachers that right. Support for that right is greatest among younger respondents; half of those under twenty-five are supportive, compared to just over one-quarter of those aged sixty-five and older. Parents and non-parents hold similar views on this issue. There is an exceptionally strong consensus among corporate executives (82 percent) that teachers not have the right to strike.

The 1996 survey also asked respondents who they think is responsible for negotiating salary contracts with high school teachers (**Table 2.15**) and who they think ideally ought to be responsible (**Table 2.16**).

TABLE 2.14
'Teachers in Ontario should have the legal right to strike.'

	Agree %	Disagree %	Neither/ not stated %	N
1980	35	56	9	1108
1982	29	63	9	1050
1984	30	55	15	1046
1986	34	54	12	1042
1988	33	58	9	1011
1990	33	58	9	1032
1992	34	56	10	1000
1994	36	57	7	1070
1996	42	52	6	1000

TABLE 2.15
'At the present time, as far as you know, which of the following is responsible for negotiating salary contracts with high school teachers?'

	%
Provincial Ministry of Education	31
Regional and local school boards	44
Principals and school councils of each school	7
Don't know	18

N=1000

TABLE 2.16
'Ideally, who do you think should be responsible for negotiating salary contracts with high school teachers?'

	%
Provincial Ministry of Education	36
Regional school boards	26
Local school boards	20
Principals and school councils of each school	11
Combinations	1
Don't know	5

N=1000

Media coverage of the release of the report on the review of Bill 100 appeared just as administration of our 1996 survey ended; thus the report itself had no influence on respondents' views. However, the commissioning of the report had occasioned some media discussion of the issues in late August and early September, before the survey began.

Over one-half of respondents are unable to identify correctly the regional and local school boards as responsible for negotiating salary contracts. About one-third think that the Ministry of Education and Training is responsible, and about one in five does not offer an opinion. Very few think that contracts are negotiated at the level of individual schools.

Parents do no better than non-parents on this question. Over one-half (56 percent) of the university educated, however, correctly identify school boards, compared to 42 percent of high school graduates and less than one-third of those who had not completed high school. Seventy percent of corporate executives also correctly identify school boards.

The distribution of views on who ought to be negotiating with high school teachers is very similar to the pattern of public perceptions on who currently undertakes the task. Preferences and perceptions are, in fact, related. Those who think that the ministry ought to be responsible are more likely to think (erroneously) that it currently is responsible. The fit is, however, by no means perfect, particularly among those who favour centralization. Thus only 44 percent of those who want the ministry to handle contract talks with teachers think that the ministry actually does so now.

Support for centralizing salary negotiations in the ministry varies with age. A majority (57 percent) of those under twenty-five want school boards to negotiate contracts. Among those forty-five and older, opinions are almost evenly divided between the ministry and boards, though slightly favouring the ministry.

Respondents who want the ministry to take over negotiations with teachers are much more likely than those who favour board-level bargaining to want to get rid of boards. However, even among those who want to centralize bargaining with the ministry, a majority (52 percent) oppose eliminating boards.

Equity

The 1996 OISE/UT survey included a series of questions concerned with equity issues in elementary and high school education, continuing themes addressed in past surveys. These include social class differences in success in school, policies to promote success of women and minority students, and affirmative action in appointing elementary

TABLE 2.17
'Do you think students from low-income families now have a better, the same or worse chance of getting a higher education as students from upper-income families?

	%
Better chance	8
About the same chance	20
Worse chance	67
Can't say	5

N=1000

school principals. We also deal in this part of the report with issues concerning business presence in schools.

Class Bias

In 1994, we asked respondents whether they thought that Ontario schools make it difficult for students from working class backgrounds to succeed.[38] A majority disagreed that this was the case. In 1996 we asked two questions in this area. The first concerned whether students from low-income families had a better or worse chance of getting a higher education than students from upper-income families. This question gauged the extent to which the public perceives the current differences in continuation rates to postsecondary education (leaving aside the issue of why these differences persist). The second question is a response to our findings in 1994. In the current survey we asked respondents not about class bias in the schools but about differences in the value that parents attach to education.

As shown in **Table 2.17**, two-thirds of respondents perceive that students from low-income families have a worse chance of getting a higher education than children from upper-income families. This view is general across social groups. Even among corporate executives, two-thirds do not dispute the existence of such inequality.

Opinions are divided over how much value low-income parents place on education for their children, compared to upper-income parents. Just over one-third of respondents think that low-income parents place less value on education; a further one-third see no difference between low- and upper-income parents, and about one in five takes the view that low-income parents place more emphasis on schooling for their children.

TABLE 2.18
'Do you think low-income parents place more, about the same, or less value on education for their children as upper-income parents?'

	More value %	About the same value %	Less value %	Can't say %	N
All respondents	22	32	36	10	1000
Schooling					
Elementary	26	47	16	12	40
High school incomplete	26	30	28	17	121
High school complete	26	37	30	7	249
Community college	28	29	35	9	207
University	16	29	46	9	366
Family income					
Under $20,000	36	30	22	12	87
$20,000–$29,999	28	40	23	10	127
$30,000–$39,999	26	24	44	6	109
$40,000–$59,999	27	32	33	8	169
$60,000–$79,999	18	33	42	7	132
$80,000 and over	13	25	54	8	161
Occupational class					
Corporate executives	11	22	60	8	114
Small employers	9	22	67	3	41
Self-employed	22	27	39	12	115
Managers	15	32	47	7	91
Professional employees	20	28	40	12	87
Supervisors	25	30	37	8	158
Service workers	25	40	28	7	109
Industrial workers	35	33	24	8	58
Homemakers	22	47	21	10	50
Unemployed	31	25	37	8	39
Retired	23	35	29	13	172
Students	23	31	38	8	50

What is most striking, however, is the extent to which respondents' views on this issue are associated with dimensions of social class: education, income, and occupation (see **Table 2.18**). The proportion of respondents who think that low-income parents value education less than better-off parents increases with educational attainment and with income. Corporate executives and small employers are much more likely than industrial and service workers to believe that this is the case. Low-income parents themselves largely reject the view that they value education for their children any less than do the more affluent; a majority

TABLE 2.19
Views on separate high schools for girls and for black students

	Agree %	Disagree %	Don't know %	N
School boards should allow separate high schools for girls where there are enough interested students.	25	66	9	1000
School boards should allow separate high schools for black students where there are enough interested students.	12	81	7	1000

of parents with family incomes of $80,000 or more believe that upper-income parents like themselves place a higher value on education.

Girls- and Blacks-Only Schools

In 1996 we asked respondents whether school boards should allow separate schools for girls and separate schools for black students where there are enough interested students. Girls-only schools have an established place both in some publicly funded Catholic school systems and among private schools (where there are also boys-only schools). The Royal Commission on Learning recommended that demonstration schools for blacks students be established.[39] Extension of girls-only schools within publicly-funded school systems and creation of schools for black students are highly contentious issues. While there has been little public discussion of these questions to date, isolated initiatives by local boards have generated considerable controversy.[40] We decided to gather base-line data on the public's views on both issues.

As **Table 2.19** indicates, while there is somewhat greater support for girls-only than for blacks-only schools, both options are rejected by a large majority of respondents. Views are generally similar across social groups; those under twenty-five are more willing than others to support girls- and blacks-only schools, but even among this group majorities currently reject these options.

Affirmative Action for Principalships

While women make up the overwhelming majority of elementary school teachers, they remain a minority among elementary school

TABLE 2.20
'Since most elementary school teachers are women, while most principals are men, at least half of future appointments of elementary school principals should go to women.'

	Agree %	Disagree %	Don't know %	N
All respondents				
1984	55	21	25	1046
1990	49	28	23	1032
1992	40	36	24	1000
1994	50	39	11	1070
1996	48	34	18	1000
Sex				
Male	42	38	21	483
Female	53	31	15	517

principals, albeit a growing one.[41] In 1996, proponents of affirmative action to remedy such situations witnessed repeal of the Employment Equity Bill, stigmatized by the government as the 'quota bill.' Women elementary teachers faced added uncertainties in the face of a likely merger between their Federation of Women Teachers' Associations of Ontario and the men's Ontario Public School Teachers' Federation, representing male teachers at the elementary level. Affirmative action is a priority for the women teachers' federation; some question whether it will have the same importance for a new, merged organization.[42]

The OISE/UT surveys have tracked opinion on affirmative action in appointments of elementary school principals since 1984. From the mid-1980s to the early 1990s we saw a decline in support for affirmative action, which was accompanied by increasing differences in the views of men and women. Surveys in 1994 and 1996 document a reversal of these trends (see **Table 2.20**). Support for affirmative action has returned to levels seen at the beginning of the decade. Differences between the views of men and of women are, however, somewhat larger in 1996 than in 1994. As in prior surveys, a large majority (66 percent) of corporate executives oppose affirmative action.

Business Presence in the Schools

Business advocacy groups have long argued that the public schools fail to represent their needs and interests adequately to students. In the

TABLE 2.21
Views on business presence in schools

	Agree %	Disagree %	Don't know %	N
Schools should give more emphasis than they do now to teaching students about the rights of business owners.				
1982	59	20	22	1050
1984	57	18	26	1046
1996	59	17	24	1000
Private corporations that loan or donate equipment to public schools should be able to advertise their products inside the school.	55	38	7	1000

current financial climate, school systems have also found themselves under pressure of another sort: to open their doors to marketing efforts by private firms that provide payments or resources to the schools.[43] In this past year, for example, a number of boards either approved or seriously considered permitting advertising on school buses.[44] In 1996, we asked for respondents' views on the representation of business views in schools and on opening schools to marketing efforts by private firms. The results are shown in **Table 2.21**.

A majority of respondents agree that schools should give more emphasis to teaching students about the rights of business owners. Views of the public in 1996 are virtually identical to those recorded in 1982 when this question was last asked. (In 1982 there was also majority support for more emphasis on the rights of workers. This question was not asked in 1996.) Parents and non-parents hold similar views on this issue. Almost three-quarters of respondents under twenty-five support the view that the rights of business owners should receive more emphasis, compared to just under half of those sixty-five or older. A surprising result is that only 36 percent of corporate executives hold this position; 43 percent were unable or unwilling to offer an opinion. This is similar to the distribution of opinion among executives in 1982.

Our marketing question offered one particular scenario in which schools might gain resources by allowing advertising. A majority of respondents are willing to allow private firms lending or donating equipment to schools to advertise their products inside the school.

Parents and non-parents hold similar views on this issue. However, older respondents are more resistant than those in younger age groups; less than half of respondents over fifty-five support allowing advertising. Corporate executives are almost equally divided: 40 percent agree that advertising should be allowed; 45 percent disagree.

3
Funding Schooling

People's willingness to pay for public services should be a basic consideration in government policy decisions. In this chapter we examine public views of educational finance. The first section deals with the public's overall budget preferences for education and includes its views on:

- budget priorities: tax cuts, deficit reduction, or maintaining services
- preferences for increased or decreased spending on education
- willingness to pay higher taxes for education

The second section covers specific issues in funding of elementary and high schools including:

- transferring tax revenue from better-off to worse-off communities
- supporting education through taxes on income rather than on property
- public funding of Catholic and private schools
- charging fees to parents for junior kindergarten
- privatizing school services

Public Funding for Education

Budget Priorities

In recent years, many Ontarians, along with other Canadians, have expressed clear support for government's reducing general spending in order to fight the deficit and the public debt.[45] There has,

TABLE 3.1
'Which of the following do you think should be the most important task for the Ontario government?'

	%
Cutting taxes	8
Reducing the deficit	29
Maintaining educational and health services	54
Combinations	7
Don't know	2

N=1000

however, been sustained majority support for maintaining specific government services, including education and job training.[46] We have found in the past that the vast majority of Ontarians would prefer to reduce spending in other areas besides education rather than increasing either deficits or taxes.[47] But in light of significant cutbacks in government services, further cuts in other services are no longer an easy option. The basic question now is whether the public wants government to maintain existing levels of services, especially in education and health, to continue the war on the deficit, or to cut taxes to try to put more money back into consumers' pockets. The general responses to this choice are summarized in **Table 3.1**.

A small majority of respondents want the Ontario government to give priority to maintaining educational and health service. More than one-quarter prefer the government to put its main emphasis on reducing the deficit. Relative support for tax cuts, which in current circumstances would probably entail further cuts in service, and not guarantee immediate deficit reductions, remains minimal, at under 10 percent. Younger people tend to be most supportive of maintaining services. Among occupational classes, there is a major difference between corporate executives' strong preference for reducing the deficit (74 percent) and professional employees' and students' desire to maintain services (70 percent).

This finding of limited support for deficit cutting in relation to other social purposes in Ontario is consistent with the results of other recent major Canadian surveys on priorities in public spending. A national poll conducted for the federal government at the end of 1995 found that majorities of Canadians preferred a budget deficit and/or higher taxes rather than cutting either health care or university education.[48] *Maclean's* magazine's 1996 year-end poll finds that Ontarians, along with most other Canadians, increasingly feel that unemployment is a more important issue than government deficits, and public resistance to further cutbacks is growing.

While there is still majority support (51 percent) for the general idea of deficit reduction at both federal and provincial levels, Ontario is most commonly regarded across the country as the province that has 'gone too far in efforts to reduce the deficit.'[49] Other Ontario polls indicate increased public perceptions of deteriorating government services, especially in hospital care, between 1993 and 1996. A recent survey in California, the home of the first successful referendum on tax cuts in North America, found that the public now favours improving public schools over cutting taxes by a ratio of almost 4 to 1 (77 percent versus 21 percent). The most recent U.S. Gallup poll on schooling also found a strong preference for improving the national education system over balancing the budget (64 percent versus 25 percent).[50] In sum, there is now quite limited popular support in Ontario and throughout North America for either deficit reduction or tax cuts at the expense of established public education and health services.

Size of Expenditures

Table 3.2 summarizes trends in the Ontario public's views on the desired sized of government spending for all purposes, for education in general, and for specific types of education. The main findings are that there is now at least plurality support for increased spending beyond the rate of inflation for all types of education, but much less support for increased general government spending. Since 1984, only about one-quarter of Ontarians have supported increased government spending, while a plurality around 40 percent have wanted government spending to keep up with inflation. Support for decreased government spending has declined from a historic high in 1994 to about one-quarter in 1996.

For the first time since 1984, public support for increased spending on education appears to have dropped slightly below 50 percent, while support for decreased spending seems to be growing and is now at 14 percent. However, both differences are still within sampling error, so no trends should yet be inferred.

Public preferences for spending on specific levels of the formal school system (elementary and high schools, community colleges,

TABLE 3.2
What would you like to see happen to government spending for the following purposes?"

	Increase %	Keep up with inflation* %	Decrease %	Not stated %	N
Total spending for all purposes					
1984	26	42	29	3	1046
1986	25	40	28	6	1042
1988	38	45	15	3	1011
1990	25	43	29	3	1032
1992	28	41	28	4	1000
1994	22	35	38	6	1070
1996	27	41	26	6	1000
For all levels of education					
1979	35	43	17	5	1084
1980	36	50	10	4	1108
1982	35	53	11	2	1050
1984	46	40	11	3	1046
1986	52	34	11	3	1042
1988	61	32	5	1	1011
1990	50	38	10	2	1032
1992	54	35	9	2	1000
1994	54	31	12	4	1070
1996	48	34	14	4	1000
For elementary and high schools					
1975†	20	51	18	10	1294
1980	38	48	10	4	1108
1982	37	50	11	3	1050
1984	45	42	10	3	1046
1986	50	36	9	5	1042
1988	61	31	5	3	1011
1990	51	39	8	2	1032
1992	55	35	8	2	1000
1994	53	33	11	4	1070
1996	47	35	13	5	1000
For community college					
1975†‡	25	45	15	14	1294
1980	37	47	10	6	1108
1982	38	48	11	4	1050
1984	48	38	10	4	1046
1986	48	35	10	7	1042
1988	55	35	6	4	1011
1990	52	35	9	4	1032
1992	55	34	8	3	1000
1994	50	33	10	8	1070
1996	45	33	13	9	1000

TABLE 3.2 (continued)

	Increase %	Keep up with inflation* %	Decrease %	Not stated %	N
For universities					
1975†‡	25	45	15	14	1294
1980	31	49	12	8	1108
1982	34	49	14	4	1050
1984	44	41	11	4	1046
1986	49	34	10	7	1042
1988	57	33	6	4	1011
1990	52	35	9	4	1032
1992	54	36	8	3	1000
1994	50	32	12	7	1070
1996	47	32	13	8	1000
For job retraining					
1984	70	19	7	3	1046
1986	73	16	8	3	1042
1988	68	24	6	3	1011
1990	66	24	7	3	1032
1992	72	19	6	3	1000
1994	64	22	10	4	1070
1996	64	19	12	6	1000
For adult training in reading and writing					
1986	71	19	6	4	1042
1988	70	22	5	3	1011
1990	68	24	5	3	1032
1992	64	28	5	4	1000
1994	63	22	8	7	1070
1996	60	24	8	8	1000

* In 1979, the middle option read, 'Maintain at about the same level' in later surveys, 'Just keep up with inflation.'
† Source: D. Auld, 'Public Sector Awareness and Preferences in Ontario,' *Canadian Tax Journal*, 27 no. 2 (March–April 1979), p. 178.
‡ Community colleges and universities combined.

and universities) have usually been similar to those for education in general and remain so. Other Canadian opinion surveys since the mid-1980s have found that a majority favour increased education funding and such attitudes now appear stronger in many other provinces than in Ontario.[51] In other countries that have experienced substantial reductions in public educational services, particularly the United Kingdom and New Zealand, public support for increased educational funding has been stronger than in Canada.[52]

48 Public Attitudes towards Education in Ontario 1996

TABLE 3.3
Preferred size of total educational expenditure by background

	Increase %	Keep up with inflation %	Decrease %	Not stated %	N
All respondents	48	34	14	4	1000
Age					
18-24	74	24	1	1	133
25-34	61	30	7	2	236
35-44	44	39	14	4	208
45-54	34	38	21	7	143
55-64	38	40	18	5	118
65+	29	37	27	6	143
Sex					
Male	43	33	20	4	483
Female	52	34	10	4	517
Occupational class					
Corporate executives	13	33	53	1	114
Small employers	42	23	33	2	41
Self-employed	38	42	15	5	115
Managers	35	43	18	4	91
Professional employees	56	30	12	2	87
Supervisors	54	35	10	1	158
Service workers	65	26	8	1	109
Industrial workers	41	36	13	9	58
Homemakers	59	25	11	5	50
Unemployed	51	34	8	7	39
Retired	38	39	18	5	172
Students	69	25	4	2	50

In Ontario support for increased spending on adult education, in the form of either job retraining or adult literacy training, remains stronger than that for devoting more money to formal schooling. Nearly two-thirds of Ontarians still want increased funding for both types of adult education.

The major social-group differences in support for education funding in Ontario are suggested by **Table 3.3**, which summarizes the differences in responses to education spending in general. Age remains the major discriminator. About three-quarters of those under twenty-five support increased spending on education, but only about one-quarter of those over sixty-five do so, and women have become more supportive than men – a possible new trend. Among occupational

TABLE 3.4
'Would you be willing to pay more taxes in support of education in Ontario/ in your community?'

	Yes %	No %	Don't know/ not stated %	N
In Ontario	50	47	3	1000
In your own community	55	42	3	1000

classes, corporate executives are distinctive in their majority support for decreased general education funding – a tendency that appears to have grown in this group over the past four years. In stark contrast, there is a continuing majority in favour of higher education spending among most categories of employees, as well as the unemployed and students. All these differences are weaker with regard to funding adult education, which attracts a majority from most groups. Even the plurality (42 percent) of people over sixty-five support increased funds for adult literacy. But only one-third of corporate executives support more funding for adult literacy or job retraining, compared to majorities in most other occupational classes.

Paying Education Taxes

The best indicator of public attitudes to education spending is probably people's personal willingness to pay higher taxes for education. As **Table 3.4** shows, the Ontario public is now quite evenly divided over willingness to pay more to support schooling in general; willingness to pay more taxes for local community schools is somewhat higher, with 55 percent now prepared to do so. This difference is similar to the difference in satisfaction with schools locally and province-wide.

As **Table 3.5** suggests, the Ontario public has remained quite evenly divided throughout the past decade on whether or not to pay more taxes in support of education. There does appear to have been a slight shift in favour of paying more personal taxes for education since the mid-1980s. Our further analyses do find a strong and growing association over the past eight years between general expressions of support for education funding and personal willingness to pay more education taxes, but not as much as comparable U.S., British, and New Zealand surveys.[53]

TABLE 3.5
Willingness to pay more taxes in support of Ontario education, by background

	Yes %	No %	Don't know/ not stated %	N
All respondents				
1984*	45	47	8	753
1988	48	48	4	1011
1990	49	46	5	1032
1994	51	47	2	1070
1996	50	47	3	1000
Age				
18-24	74	19	8	133
25-34	60	38	2	236
35-44	52	44	4	208
45-54	46	53	1	143
55-64	30	69	1	118
65+	33	63	4	143
Occupational class				
Corporate executives	22	75	3	114
Small employers	46	54	0	41
Self-employed	45	53	3	115
Managers	46	53	1	91
Professional employees	62	37	1	87
Supervisors	60	38	2	158
Service workers	54	39	6	109
Industrial workers	50	45	5	58
Homemakers	42	58	0	50
Unemployed	44	44	12	39
Retired	39	57	4	172
Students	80	11	9	50

* From the CEA's 1984 poll of Canadian opinion on education; see George Flower, *Speaking Out* (Toronto: Canadian Education Association, 1984).

Table 3.5 further shows that some of the social groups most opposed to education spending in general are also the most unwilling to pay more personal taxes. The majority of younger people are willing to pay more taxes for education, while only about one-third of those over fifty-five are. Corporate executives are again distinctive in their strong majority opposition to paying more for education. Smaller majorities of small employers, managers, and the self-employed, as well as retirees and homemakers, also now appear opposed, while small majorities in most employee classes are now supportive; but

TABLE 3.6
'Tax money should be transferred from better-off communities to the less well-off communities so that money spent on each student is about the same across the province.'

	%
Agree	79
Disagree	13
Don't know	8

N=1000

these differences are only marginal, and most groups remain quite divided. In stark contrast to corporate executives, students – who have the least present capacity to pay – express the strongest willingness. The lowest-income groups are generally now just as willing as higher-income groups to pay more taxes for education.

Funding of Elementary and High Schools

Redistribution of Education Taxes

Achievement of the principle of equitable funding for all school students across the province was a key recommendation of the Royal Commission on Learning.[54] **Table 3.6** shows that public support for this principle is now very strong. About four-fifths of the public agrees that funds should be transferred from better-off to less well-off communities to achieve such equity. There is a virtually total consensus across all social groupings and regions. The more difficult question is what revenue sources should be used both to fund schooling and to achieve such equitable per-student distribution.

Property versus Income Taxes

The main revenue-sources issue for many years has been whether provincial taxes should replace local property taxes as the primary source of school funding. Major government commissions in 1985 and 1993 recommended such changes.[55] Both the 1993 provincial commission and more recent province-appointed bodies have recommended the pooling and equitable distribution of industrial and commercial property taxes across school boards for education funding.[56] Both our own and other opinion surveys have found majority support

TABLE 3.7
'Local property taxes for schools should be replaced with an income tax for schools.'

	Agree %	Disagree %	Can't say %	N
All respondents				
1990*	36	40	24	1032
1994	34	43	23	1070
1996	34	31	35	1000

* The 1990 question wording differed slightly.

for this proposition over the past six years.[57] The larger and more controversial issue is whether provincial income taxes should replace local residential property taxes for school funding. While the 1993 commission recommended this, a mid-1996 report to the minister on reform of education finance failed to make any recommendation on the matter;[58] in September 1996, the minister announced yet another committee to study the issue and then stated that property taxes for schooling could soon be replaced by provincial income taxes in a major school overhaul that would also see the elimination or drastic scaling back of school boards.[59] It was in this immediate context that our question on the issue was asked. Since 1990 we have tracked public preferences on this question. The results are summarized in **Table 3.7**

The general Ontario public remains both divided and increasingly uncertain about the relative merits of property and provincial income taxes for funding education. The public is now about evenly split into three categories: those who support relying on provincial income tax for school funding, those who disagree, and those who are uncertain.[60] The main change over the past two years has been a reduction in definite disagreement with using income taxes and a corresponding increase in uncertainty about preferred sources of school revenue. Neither the several recent committee reports nor the minister's comments appear to have led to either greater public support or greater public clarity on the issue to date.

Virtually all social groups are now quite divided on replacing local property taxes with provincial income taxes for school funding. The level of uncertainty among all groups is unprecedented in any of our prior surveys. Clearly, there is a need for fuller public debate prior to any major policy change.

Funding for Catholic and Private Schools

Public funding of Catholic high schools was extended from Grade 10 to the end of high school by the Ontario provincial government in 1984. Since then, the issue of what types of schools should be given government funding has generally focused on possible extension of public funding to various private schools; public debate about funding private religious schools continued up to a negative Supreme Court of Canada decision in November, 1996.[61] However, a 1995 referendum supporting establishment of a public school system in Newfoundland, where denominational schools had previously made up the entire system, and subsequent government initiatives to amend the constitution to achieve this result have led to growing expressions of public concern by Catholic leaders about diminished protection for Ontario's separate schools.[62] Also, in the midst of the present survey, the report of a major Quebec commission recommended taking religion out of the schools and sharply reducing government funding for private schools in that province.[63]

Since 1984, we have regularly asked respondents to express their preferences on the full range of possible options, from funding only public schools to funding all types of private schools. The main findings are summarized in **Table 3.8**. The Ontario public seems to be becoming more divided in its views about extended funding. Nearly 40 percent would now prefer only public schools to receive government funding, one-third prefer the current status of full funding for both public and Catholic schools, and more than one-quarter want public funding extended as well either to religious or to all private schools. Support for limiting government funding only to public schools has increased significantly in the 1990s, while support for full Catholic funding has declined. Support for options that include funding of private schools has remained very stable, at around 27 percent, since 1984. In any case, advocates of a unitary public system should note that the funding of Catholic schools, alone or with private schools, still has majority support (60 percent).

Views on extended public funding have become increasingly divided by religious affiliation. There is growing majority support for funding only public schools among the increasing numbers with no religion, as well as growing plurality support among other non-Catholics. A majority of Catholics continue to favour funding of

TABLE 3.8
'What schools do you think should be given government funding, provided that they meet province-wide standards?'

	Public only %	Public and Catholic as now %	Public, Catholic, and private religious %	Public, Catholic, and all private %	Don't know %	N
All respondents						
1984	21	51	9	17	2	1046
1986	28	40	7	23	2	1042
1988	24	41	7	21	8	1011
1992	33	36	10	18	3	1000
1994	36	31	4	24	5	1052
1996	38	33	4	23	3	1000
Religion						
Protestant	48	26	3	21	3	458
Catholic	12	54	5	26	2	317
Jewish	45	7	15	33	0	12
Other	45	13	16	27	0	20
No religion	57	20	2	18	3	142

Catholic schools and very few support a unitary school system. Not surprisingly, support for these various options is stronger among those who have children in the respective types of schools; for example, most of the tiny minority who now have children in private schools support public funding of these schools.

But prior surveys have found strong majority support for sharing resources between public and Catholic school boards under tight budget conditions.[64] In further analysis of the present survey, we find that majorities both of those who prefer to fund only public schools (62 percent) and of those who want to fund both public and Catholic *schools* (52 percent) now support merging public and Catholic school *boards*. There is now general agreement on having fewer school boards regardless of which types of schools people think should be funded.

Fees for Junior Kindergarten

With tight government budgets, user fees have been suggested as a means of continuing to provide various public services. In the wake of the provincial government's definitive rejection of the Royal

TABLE 3.9
'Parents should be charged for sending their children to junior kindergarten, the same as they are for child care.'

	%
Agree	46
Disagree	46
Don't know	8

N=1000

TABLE 3.10
'School boards in your community should contract with private businesses to provide transportation, janitors and food services for schools rather than having these services provided by school board employees.'

	%
Agree	53
Disagree	31
Don't know	16

N=1000

Commission on Learning's recommendation to extend and fund early childhood education, and its decision to make junior kindergarten optional, user fees for junior kindergarten have become a serious policy matter at the local level in Ontario. Current public views are summarized in **Table 3.9**.

Ontarians are very evenly divided on whether or not parents should be charged users' fees for junior kindergarten. Those who favour early childhood education are much more likely (60 percent) to oppose user fees than others. Younger people and those with young children are certainly less supportive of user fees. But most social groups are internally split on this issue.

Privatizing School Services

Another option increasingly being considered across Canada is contracting out some school services to private firms. Ancillary services such as transportation, janitorial, and food services have been supplied for decades in the United States by private firms in many schools, and charter schools are now being tested in many states. In Canada, ancillary services have been contracted out only in a few places, and charter schools have only recently been approved in Alberta.[65] The 1996 U.S. Gallup poll on schooling found that at least three-quarters of respondents supported contracting with local businesses to provide each of these ancillary services but that only one-third supported businesses' running the entire operation.[66] We have asked a similar question vis-à-vis Ontario. The results appear in **Table 3.10**.

A small majority of Ontario's public now favours contracting out transportation, janitorial, and food services, with about one-third definitely opposed and the remainder uncertain. Not surprisingly, support is substantially lower than in the United States where the practice is much more extensive. The main group differences are by occupational class, with corporate executives, small employers, and the self-employed strongly in favour and employee groups generally divided. Women are more likely than men to disagree.

4
Postsecondary Education

In December 1996 Ontario's Advisory Panel on Future Directions for Postsecondary Education submitted its report, *Excellence, Accessibility and Responsibility*, to the minister of education and training. The report makes eighteen recommendations covering funding levels for the postsecondary sector, tuition fees, student assistance, roles (including credentials offered) and links among universities and colleges, roles for private universities, and faculty evaluation.

In this chapter we take up many of these issues addressed by the Advisory Panel's recommendations. The first section focuses on access and organization; the second takes up funding issues. The OISE/UT surveys have tracked opinion over a number of years on the importance of postsecondary education, accessibility and funding. The 1996 survey examines key issues in the university sector. In 1992 and 1994, however, the focus was on the colleges of applied arts and technology (CAATs). At the end of the first section we append a short review of the findings of the earlier surveys that bear on the Advisory Panel's recommendations for the college sector.

The first section of this chapter deals with organization and reorganization of the postsecondary sector:

- the importance that the public attaches to postsecondary education
- program quotas linked to availability of jobs for graduates
- limiting access to postsecondary education for budget reasons
- maintaining or changing the number of universities in Ontario
- maintaining or changing the number of programs offered by each university
- allowing private universities
- college issues, including roles and links to the university sector

TABLE 4.1
'In your opinion, how important is a university or college education today?'

	1979* %	1986 %	1992 %	1994 %	1996 %
Very important	34	61	75	70	69
Fairly important	40	30	21	25	26
Not too important	23	7	3	4	4
Don't know	3	2	1	1	1
	N=1080	N=1042	N=1000	N=1070	N=1000

* Ontario Ministry of Education, *Attitudes of the Public towards Schools in Ontario* (Toronto: MOE, 1979).

The second section covers funding issues:

- preferred responses to budget cuts: rationing, fee increases, or program cuts
- dividing of tuition costs between government and students
- increasing tuition fees for professional programs
- affect of higher fees on students from low-income families
- income-contingent repayment of student loans
- funding for university research

Reorganization

The Importance of Postsecondary Education

In the first half of the 1980s both Canadians and Americans drastically, and it seems permanently, re-evaluated their views on the value of postsecondary education. In 1979, a survey sponsored by the Ontario Ministry of Education asked a representative sample of Ontarians how important they thought a university or college education was. About one-third thought it was very important. By 1986, when the sixth OISE/UT survey repeated this question, the proportion had increased to 61 percent. An almost identical increase was recorded by the U.S. Gallup poll over the same period.[67] By 1992, three-quarters of Ontarians thought that getting a university or college education was very important; this proportion has dropped somewhat to about 70 percent in 1994 and 1996 (see **Table 4.1**).

Confirmation of a new public awareness of the value of postsecondary education is provided by views on how much education a per-

TABLE 4.2
'How much education do you think a person needs in order to get along in this society?'

	1988 %		1996 %	
Elementary	2		2	
Some high school	n.a.		1	
A high school diploma	n.a.	33	27	30
Vocational high school	8		n.a.	
Academic high school	23		n.a.	
Community college or trade school	40		39	
Undergraduate university degree	11		19	
Graduate university degree	13		6	
Can't say	3		7	
	N=1011		N=1000	

n.a. = not asked

son now needs 'to get along.' In both 1988, when the question was first asked, and 1996 almost two-thirds of respondents indicate that education beyond high school (trade school, college, or university) is needed; about one-quarter cite university (see **Table 4.2**). Attitudes on both the importance of postsecondary education and the amount of education needed to get along in this society are similar across social groups.

Creation of CAATs and expansion of universities in the 1960s vastly increased access to postsecondary education. Public support for open access, particularly as against restrictions based on perceived labour force needs, extends back at least to the early 1980s. As indicated in **Table 4.3**, between 1979 and 1996 a majority of the public has consistently opposed limiting program enrolments according to availability of jobs for graduates. Rejection of restriction on access based on availability of jobs is general across social groups.

In 1992 and 1994, majorities also rejected restrictions on accessibility to college programs on financial grounds (see **Table 4.4**). Between 1992 and 1994, however, the segment of the public willing to accept such restrictions increased. When in 1996, we asked whether every qualified person who wanted to attend university should be guaranteed a place, even if this meant higher spending on universities, opinion was almost equally divided.

There are significant differences in views on guaranteed access if this requires higher spending. Women are more likely to be supportive under these conditions than are men (51 versus 42 percent). Those

TABLE 4.3
'The number of students admitted to university and community college programmes should be based primarily on the availability of jobs for graduates, even if this keeps out qualified students who want these programs.'

	Agree %	Disagree %	Neither/ not stated %	N
All respondents				
1979	37	53	10	1084
1982	37	52	11	1050
1986	25	61	14	1042
1988	19	64	18	1011
1990	25	64	12	1032
1994	32	61	7	1070
1996	32	60	7	1000

TABLE 4.4
'Every qualified person who wants to attend university [community college] should be guaranteed a place even if this means spending more tax money on the universities [colleges].'

	Agree %	Disagree %	Neither/ not stated %	N
Community college				
1992	58	29	13	1000
1994	53	40	7	1070
University				
1996	48	44	9	1000

over fifty-five are less supportive than younger respondents. Just over one-half of the university educated (51 percent) reject guaranteed access if this may entail higher expenditures; narrow majorities (50–58 percent) in all other educational categories support it. Views of parents and non-parents are similar. There is a strong consensus among corporate executives; almost two-thirds reject guaranteed access, while only one-quarter are supportive.

Expansion and Differentiation

The Advisory Panel's report notes that government policy (regardless of party affiliation) since the 1960s has been not to support establishment of new universities. Legislation in 1983 codified traditional

TABLE 4.5
The Ontario government is currently considering a reorganization of the university system. In your opinion, what should be done in each of the following areas:'

	Increase %	Stay the same %	Decrease %	Can't say %	N
Should the number of universities...?					
1984	19	72	7	2	1046
1996	20	68	6	7	1000
Should the number of programs offered at each university ...?					
1984	33	55	7	5	1046
1996	26	47	17	11	1000

practice that no institution could designate itself a university and grant degrees without a charter from the provincial legislature.[68] As shown in **Table 4.5**, public opinion currently supports a freeze on new universities and may have done so for over a decade. In both 1984 and 1996, over two-thirds of respondents to the OISE/UT survey indicated that in any reorganization of the university system the number of institutions should remain the same. At the same time, this implies resistance to a reduction in the number of universities either through withdrawing charters or amalgamation. In both 1984 and 1996, about one in five favours more universities, while fewer than one in 10 supports reducing their number. Views are similar across social groups, though corporate executives are somewhat more likely (19 percent) to favour decreasing numbers than the general public.

On differentiation, the Advisory Panel observes:

The servant of quality is specialization, requiring differentiation among our institutions. We cannot expect all to be excellent in everything. We cannot support them as though they were. This is why we do not look for grand designs. Pushing institutions into prescribed boxes is not the route to quality. We believe profoundly that our postsecondary institutions need to have the room to experiment, to abandon what they cannot do well enough, and to concentrate their resources in areas in which they can ... Equally important for both governments and institutional leaders is that rewards must go to those who succeed and not to those who fail.[69]

The panel states its support for continuing a dual-track postsecondary system (with distinct college and university sectors) and recommends a limited role for private universities. (Both these issues are taken up below.) It makes no recommendations, however, about differentiation among publicly funded universities. Put differently, there is no recommendation for formalizing a differentiation of university missions that would reserve large-scale research and doctoral studies to a core set of institutions, with the remainder concentrating on undergraduate teaching. The report explicitly rejects a regulatory regime or 'grand design' of 'prescribed boxes.' However, the panel appears to favour and expect more differentiation rather than less. It desires that 'a hundred flowers blossom' out of initiatives from institutions themselves but that the province act as a highly selective gardener, providing growing room only for the best. Out of this process universities would become more differentiated; most would have no more and perhaps fewer programs than they offer now.

In 1984 and 1996 we have asked respondents what should happen to the number of programs offered at each university. In 1996, as in 1984, the overwhelming majority continue to favour either maintaining numbers or increasing offerings (see **Table 4.5**). The results suggest, however, some growing support for reducing the number of programs offered at each institution (probably accompanied by specialization). Compared to 1984, fewer respondents now favour either an increase in the number of programs offered or the status quo; almost one in five would now like to see a reduction in programs offered at each institution, compared to 7 percent in 1984.

Views are similar across social groups. The university educated, however, are more polarized than other categories: about one-quarter want more programs (similar to other educational groups) and about the same proportion favour a decrease (higher than for other groups). Corporate executives hold much more distinct views: almost one-half (46 percent) want fewer programs at each university; only one-quarter opt for the status quo, while one in 10 favours an increase.

Private Universities

The final recommendation of the Advisory Panel is a limited role for privately funded, not-for-profit universities in Ontario. Of the non-financial recommendations, this is likely to generate the most controversy. The recommendation sets out conditions and standards designed to preclude 'degree mills.' Moreover, students would not be eligible for grants but would have access to student loans on the same

TABLE 4.6
Views on allowing private universities in Ontario

	Yes %	No %	Can't say %	N
Should Ontario allow private universities to be established?	62	32	6	1000
... even if the tuition fees charged are several times higher than those for publicly funded universities?	50	42*	8	1000
... even if they are eligible for public funding for student aid and research?	30	59*	11	1000

* Includes those who oppose private universities in general and those whose opposition is due to the stated condition, i.e., higher tuition fees or eligibility for public funds.

basis as students in publicly funded universities. Private institutions would presumably be eligible for government research grants and contracts.

The OISE/UT survey included three related questions on privately funded universities in an attempt to capture at least some of the complexities of the issue. It first asked simply whether Ontario should allow private universities. Those who said 'yes' were asked two additional questions: whether such universities should be permitted even if they charged much higher tuition fees than publicly funded institutions and even if they would be eligible for public funding for student aid and research. In **Tables 4.6** and **4.7**, results for all three questions are based on the full sample. In reporting the results of the follow-up question, we have added those who said 'no' to the initial, unqualified question to the 'no' group for each of the follow-up questions. Thus **Table 4.6** shows how many additional 'no' votes are registered by each of the two qualifications. (This also applies to 'can't say.')[70]

As **Table 4.6** indicates, initial public reaction to private universities is positive. Almost two-thirds say 'yes' to our initial question. Adding the qualification that tuition fees are several times higher reduces support, but one-half of respondents overall remain in favour.[71] Eligibility for public funds has more effect on respondents' positions: less than one-third would allow private universities in Ontario if they had access to public funding for student aid and for research.

Initial support for private universities is general across social groups. However, a smaller majority of women (55 percent) than men

TABLE 4.7
Views on allowing private universities by sex and educational attainment

	If higher tuition fees % yes	If eligible for public funds % yes	N
Sex			
Male	59	32	483
Female	42	27	517
Education			
Elementary	37	17	40
Secondary incomplete	35	23	121
Secondary complete	44	30	249
Community college	55	32	207
University	59	32	366

(70 percent) favour them. Support also increases with income; just over one-half of those with family incomes under $30,000 would allow them compared to three-quarters of those earning $80,000 or more.

Differences by gender and income also emerge when the issue is qualified in terms of higher tuition fees.[72] Now, however, educational attainment makes a difference in views. **Table 4.7** shows the extent of opposition by education; among those with less than a high school diploma, just over one-third continue to support private universities. Majorities of those with postsecondary education remain in favour, while high school graduates divide about equally. There are also differences by occupational class. Three-quarters of corporate executives and small employers remain in favour, compared to about one-half of most other occupational groups. The unemployed and the retired are less likely to be supportive. Students are about equally divided.

Access to public funding redefines the issue across social groups. Differences by gender, income, and education (particularly excluding the small group with elementary schooling only) largely disappear. Among corporate executives, consensus on allowing private universities gives way to an almost even division of opinion, with 47 percent supportive, and 41 percent opposed.

The College Sector and Sectoral Links: Findings from 1990, 1992, and 1994[73]

The Advisory Panel makes a number of recommendations regarding the college sector and its relationship to the universities. It affirms the dual structure of postsecondary education (without formalizing this as a recommendation). Formal recommendations allow colleges more latitude to assume a province-wide mandate without abandoning their obligations to serve their local communities; see greater government sponsorship of credit transfer and cooperative programming between colleges and universities; see development of a unique college credential; and restrict degree-granting status to universities, with perhaps some colleges eventually becoming degree-granting polytechnics and ultimately universities.

The 1992 and 1994 surveys indicated that the public saw colleges as having a distinctive mandate. Most respondents in both years saw the future of the colleges in terms of their continuing to develop applied professional and technical education. Only minorities wanted them instead to take on roles similar to U.S junior colleges by offering more general arts and science programs. (Support for a junior college-type role, however, increased from 25 percent in 1992 to 36 percent in 1994.)

In 1994, we asked respondents about the geographical focus of colleges' mandates. If a trade-off had to be made, should colleges give priority to training for jobs in their local communities or for jobs across Ontario. Almost two-thirds of respondents gave priority to a provincial mandate. This is consistent with the panel's recommendation that government-defined catchment areas for each college be abandoned.

While the public regards the colleges as holding a distinct mandate, there is also support both for credit transfers and cooperative programming. In 1990, the overwhelming majority (74 percent) favoured making it easier for students to transfer course credits from college to university. In 1994, two-thirds favoured collaboration between colleges and universities if new degree programs were to be offered in applied professional and technical education.

Funding Choices

We documented the extent of general public support for government spending on postsecondary education in the previous chapter. Here the focus is on funding choices faced by these institutions and their students, with particular attention to universities.

Fee Hikes versus Cutbacks

In the context of continuing constraints in federal and provincial allocations, universities and colleges have been compelled to consider carefully what other options they have to deliver their programs

TABLE 4.8
'With government budgets tight, universities [community colleges] may be faced with the choice of limiting enrolment, reducing program services or increasing fees. What choice do you favour?'

	Colleges 1992 %	Colleges 1994 %	Universities 1996 %
Increase fees	44	56	32
Limit enrolment	28	19	34
Reduce services/programs	19	13	20
Don't know	10	13	14
	N=1000	N=1070	N=1000

and services. The basic choices within their direct control are to increase student fees to maintain services; to limit enrolments in order to provide adequate service to smaller numbers with diminished resources; or to cut programs that they can no longer adequately provide. Private fund-raising remains a secondary option for most public institutions.

Ontario's universities and colleges have responded with fee increases and selective program cuts and quotas. Universities have also made particular use of early retirement packages. Tuition rates at all Canadian universities have increased significantly over the past decade both in absolute terms and as a proportion of the total cost.[74] In the past three academic years, Ontario's increases in university fees have led the nation, with the highest jumps coming in September 1996, including a 10 percent increase imposed by the provincial government and discretionary additions of another 10 percent, which most universities chose to add.[75] Some universities have limited enrolment or eliminated programs, but such efforts remain much more variable both within and between institutions. Which response does the public favour? We have asked this question for colleges in 1992 and 1994 and for universities in the present survey. The results appear in **Table 4.8**.

The Ontario public currently holds mixed views on this issue. About one-third favour enrolment limits, another one-third prefer fee increases, about one-fifth would opt for reducing programs, and the remainder remain uncertain. The three options are not mutually exclusive, as the recent decisions of these institutions demonstrate, so finding mixed public views is not surprising. The 1992 and 1994 findings for colleges are not directly comparable with these 1996

TABLE 4.9
'The government's share of the cost of educating a university student is decreasing so that now students pay about one-third of the cost of their education. What amount of the cost of a university student's education should be paid for by the government and what amount by the student?'

	%
Government should pay all	4
Government should pay 2/3	25
Both should pay half	48
Student should pay 2/3	12
Student should pay all	6
Can't say	6

N=1000

university findings. But the differences do suggest that actual fee increases may have diminished support for further fee increases and greater support for enrolment or program cutbacks.

The major background difference is related to family income. Only one-fifth of those in families with incomes under $20,000 support fee increases, while a strong plurality (46 percent) of those in families earning more than $80,000 do so. Among occupational classes, corporate executives are the strongest supporters of fee increases (47 percent) and least likely to opt for limiting enrolment (16 percent); conversely, students themselves are least likely to prefer fee increases (16 percent) and most likely to choose enrolment limits (56 percent). Women are also less likely to choose fee increases (26 percent) than men (37 percent) are.

Cost Sharing by Government and Students

The actual funding of students' postsecondary education involves several components, including federal transfer funds, provincial grants to institutions, university general funds and student awards, government and private scholarships, student loans, student earnings and parental contributions.[76] The basic public policy choices revolve around relative emphasis on government support and on students' own contributions. The 1996 OISE/UT survey intends to establish a benchmark of public views on this issue. Given the complexities of both public and private/personal funding, expressions of preferred proportioning should not be taken very precisely but as indications of general priorities. For the basic findings see **Table 4.9**.

There appears to be general public support for students' assuming more of the cost of their university education. Nearly one-half of Ontarians currently feel that government and students should share costs about equally. About 30 percent think that the government should contribute a higher share, while less than 20 percent feel that the student should pay more than half the cost. Equal sharing is the plurality view in nearly all social groups. The most notable exception is francophones, a small majority of whom (51 percent) think that the government should pay more than half the cost. Views are also related to family income, with a plurality of those in the poorest families (47 percent) wanting the government to pay more than half the costs; but even in families with incomes over $80,000 there is very little support (19 percent) for students' paying more than half the costs.

Increases in Tuition Fees

The report of the Advisory Panel on Directions for Postsecondary Education states as 'a general principle': 'Postsecondary education must evolve in a way which provides the opportunity for a high-quality learning experience to every Ontarian who is motivated to seek it and who has the ability to pursue it.'[77] However the panel's recommendations concerning tuition fees, student assistance, and student loans amount in effect to transfer of costs from governments to students. The panel does not take up the debate concerning the impact of higher tuition fees and debt loads on participation rates of children from lower-income families (or on adults with low incomes).

While there may now be general public support for increasing students' share of the costs of postsecondary education, among the related issues that have recently raised public concern are the extent of tuition fee increases and their social consequences. Should there be differential fee increases for professional degree programs? Will significant general fee increases keep students from low-income families out of university? Our findings on these questions are summarized in **Table 4.10**.

A small majority of Ontarians support the proposition that professional degree programs such as medicine, dentistry, business, and law should be able to charge higher tuition fees because their graduates will probably be able to earn more money; about 40 percent are opposed, and less than 10 percent are uncertain. Francophones are most likely to oppose such differential fees (57 percent). Women

TABLE 4.10
Views on university tuition fees

	Agree %	Disagree %	Can't say %	N
Universities should be able to charge higher tuition fees for professional degree programs such as medicine, dentistry, business and law because these graduates will probably earn more money.	53	39	8	1000
Increasing university tuition fees by half will prevent students from low-income families from going to university.	64	29	8	1000

are less likely to agree (47 percent) than men (60 percent). Among occupational classes, corporate executives are probably the strongest supporters of differential fees (68 percent), but about one-half of those in most other classes, including students (52 percent), also favour them.

There is general consensus that substantial increases in tuition fees would prevent students from low-income families from going to university. About two-thirds of Ontarians agree with this statement, while less than one-third disagree. This attitude is widely shared across virtually all social groups; it is even the plurality view among corporate executives (49 percent), who are least likely to agree.

Differential Student Assistance

What forms of student assistance would Ontarians like to see, given that they tend to support both general and differential student fee increases, and also generally recognize that increased fees present significant barriers to low-income students? The most evident policy options are probably preferential financial assistance for low-income students and income-contingent repayment of student loans. The Advisory Panel has made recommendations supporting both types of plans.[78] The results of our questions on these issues are presented in **Table 4.11**.

There is overwhelming support for such differential plans. Well over 80 percent approve of both financial assistance to low-income students and loan repayments contingent on students' earnings after graduation. The vast majority in all social groups appear to regard such measures as good means for improving economic fairness in postsecondary education in a situation of fast-rising student debt

TABLE 4.11
Views on student assistance

	Agree %	Disagree %	Can't say %	N
The government should provide more assistance to high school students with the ability and desire to attend university but not enough money.	85	11	4	1000
How quickly students have to repay their student loans should be tied to their income after graduation, with higher earners paying off loans faster.	88	8	4	1000

loads.[79] We have rarely found such unanimity on any educational issue.

Funding University Research

Research is generally recognized as 'an integral part of the functioning of all universities.'[80] Advocates have expressed concern that budget cuts jeopardize this function, while critics note the lack of coherent research policies and evident practical relevance. The extent of public support for funding research at Ontario universities is suggested by the results in **Table 4.12**.

TABLE 4.12
'What would you like to see happen to funding for research at Ontario universities over the next 5 years?'

	Increase %	Not change %	Decrease %	Can't say %	N
All respondents	55	36	5	4	1000
Schooling					
Elementary	22	51	17	10	40
High school incomplete	46	45	3	6	121
High school complete	51	43	4	3	249
Community college	57	33	6	4	207
University	63	29	4	4	366

A definite majority (55 percent) of Ontarians now favour increased funding for research at Ontario universities, while over one-third want to see current funding levels maintained and only 5 percent support decreased funding. There is majority support across most social groups for increased funding. The major difference is by respondents' formal schooling. The more schooling people have, the more likely they are to support more funding; only among the small number with elementary schooling is there any significant support for decreased spending on university research.

5
Education and Work: Perceptions and Policies

Relations between education and work have become increasingly problematic in recent years, with significant changes in both institutional spheres and frequent criticisms of how each sphere is failing to respond to changes in the other.[81] From its inception, and especially in 1986, 1990, and 1994, the OISE/UT survey has assessed public opinion on key aspects of these links. The present survey tracks trends in personal and general perceptions of the relations between workplaces and education and preferences on alternative policies on education-work linkage.

The first section of this chapter, dealing with perceptions on education and work, includes the following issues:

- personal perceptions of underused skills in individuals' own jobs
- personal feelings of entitlement to a better job based on individuals' own educational attainments
- the match between education and jobs in the general workforce
- main causes of unemployment
- unemployment of university graduates compared to high school graduates
- likelihood that university graduates will get better jobs
- general job prospects

The second section deals with four policy issues concerning education and work:

- workfare versus skills training for welfare recipients
- Canadian spending levels for research and development

TABLE 5.1
'Do you have some skills from your experience and training that you would like to be using in your work, but can't use on your present job?'

	Yes %	No %	Can't say %	N
All employed respondents				
1994	41	56	3	702
1996	40	56	4	658
Age				
18-24	50	49	1	74
25-34	48	49	3	199
35-44	33	64	3	177
45-54	36	58	6	118
55-64	29	59	11	63
Schooling				
Elementary	24	76	0	9
High school incomplete	31	66	3	63
High school complete	35	61	5	163
Community college	39	55	6	159
University	45	52	3	255

- job creation through a shorter standard workweek
- job creation through a lower minimum wage for youth

Perceptions

Underused Skills

The 1994 OISE/UT survey found that nearly three-quarters of employed Ontarians perceived themselves to be adequately qualified for their current jobs, while about one-fifth felt that they were overqualified and only 5 percent believed themselves underqualified. All our surveys since 1984 have found that, according to self reports, around one-fifth of Ontario's labour force is overqualified in terms of the level of formal schooling required for entry.[82] In the last two surveys we have probed further to determine the extent to which people have relevant skills that they cannot use on their current jobs. The findings are summarized in **Table 5.1**.

In both 1994 and 1996, the majority respond that they do not have other relevant skills that they would like to use at work. But about 40 percent of the members of employed workforce continue to say that they have other skills that they would like to use. This sense of unused skills is stronger among both younger and more highly schooled workers. It is lower among corporate executives (19 percent) than other occupational classes. Visible-minority workers, who tend to be both younger and more highly schooled than workers in general, have the highest sense of unused work skills (about 60 percent). Overall, the results continue to offer an explicit indication of substantial underuse of existing job skills in Ontario.

Deserving a Better Job

When underemployment was first identified as a significant phenomenon in the late 1960s,[83] there was much speculation that the social protest in that period by highly schooled youths was fuelled by a sense of entitlement to better jobs than they were likely to get. Later research has not found a general connection between underemployment and critical political views.[84] Sceptics have argued that 'underemployment' is merely a conceptual artefact and that people generally just try to get as much schooling as they can to compete in an increasingly highly schooled labour force. In any case, if there were a widespread attitude that people's schooling entitled them to better jobs, this would be an indicator of significant pressure for workplace reforms. Since 1986, the OISE/UT survey has tracked this sense of entitlement among Ontario workers. The basic results appear in **Table 5.2**.

About one-half of workers now disagree with the notion that they are entitled to a better job, while about one-third believe themselves so entitled and the remaining 15 percent are uncertain. There appears to have been a small recent decline in the proportion who agree that they are entitled to a better job and some increase in dissent from this view. This sense of entitlement remains related to age, with majorities in all age groups over thirty-five rejecting the notion; agreement is highest among those eighteen to twenty-four, but has dropped from 72 percent in 1994 to 46 percent in this survey.

Income and occupational differences are notable at the extremes. Those in the lowest-income families are very likely to feel that they deserve better jobs, while those in the highest-income families generally dissent. Corporate executives are virtually unanimous in their dissent, while students and the unemployed strongly agree. Visible-minority workers have consistently expressed a stronger agreement (58 percent) than do those in other ethnic groups. However, in terms of general levels of schooling, those with university attainments are

TABLE 5.2
'With the level of schooling I have, I am entitled to a better job than I have been able to get.'

	Agree %	Disagree %	Can't say %	N
All employed respondents				
1986	31	44	25	643
1988	35	46	19	627
1990	38	44	19	656
1994	39	46	15	716
1996	34	51	15	666
Age				
18–24	46	37	17	78
25–34	43	41	16	199
35–44	34	53	13	179
45–54	22	66	13	119
55–64	24	68	8	63
Family income				
Under $20,000	78	13	9	31
$20,000–29,999	43	52	6	73
$30,000–39,999	41	46	13	68
$40,000–59,999	36	45	19	133
$60,000–79,999	35	52	14	110
$80,000 and over	22	65	13	136

apparently now no more likely (32 percent) than high school graduates (38 percent) to agree. Overall, there has been a growing tendency of late, particularly among young people, to be content to have any kind of job and a somewhat diminished dissatisfaction at not having a better one.

Enough Education?

Whatever their personal experience in linking their own education and work, our prior surveys have found that most Ontarians believe that more skill is involved in the work of today than of a generation ago.[85] But what about general perceptions of the current links between work and education? Does the public think that people in general have more education than the jobs require, the right amount, or too little? The responses for 1994 and 1996 are summarized in **Table 5.3**.

Ontarians are now quite divided, with about one-third thinking that people have more education than required, about one-quarter feeling

76 Public Attitudes towards Education in Ontario 1996

TABLE 5.3
'Do you think that people generally have more education than their jobs require, the right amount or too little?'

	1994 %	1996 %
More	40	35
Right amount	27	26
Too little	25	30
Can't say	8	9

N=1000

that most people have the right amount, and just under one-third believing most people have too little. There has been a slight tendency away from 'more' to 'too little' over the past two years. These divisions prevail across nearly all social groups. Corporate executives are least likely to think that people have more education than their jobs require (14 percent).

Causes of Unemployment

Respondents have been asked in both 1994 and 1996 about their views of the main cause of unemployment among young people. As **Table 5.4** shows, the majority see the major cause as an economy that is not generating enough jobs for young people. About one-fifth think that schools are not preparing students well enough for jobs, and another one-fifth, that the main cause is lack of motivation. The main recent change is more people blaming the economy and fewer blaming young people themselves. The unemployed (79 percent) and students (73 percent) remain most likely to focus on the economy, which has

TABLE 5.4
'Which of the following do you think is the most important cause of unemployment among young people?'

	1994 %	1996 %
The economy is not generating enough jobs	50	58
Schools are not preparing students well enough for jobs	21	20
Many young people do not want to work	25	18
Can't say	3	4

N=1000

TABLE 5.5
Views on employment prospects for university graduates

	Agree %	Disagree %	Can't say %	N
A university graduate is as likely to be unemployed as a high school graduate.				
1982	63	31	6	1050
1994	62	34	4	1070
1996	60	34	5	1000
A university graduate is more likely to obtain a better job which pays a higher income than a high school graduate.				
1996	84	12	4	1000

become the majority response in all occupational categories. There is now relatively little inclination to blame the schools.

Current Job Prospects

In the context of persistent high levels of youth unemployment, public perceptions of the relative employment prospects of youths with different levels of schooling are also relevant. In 1982 and again in the last two surveys, we have asked whether people think that university graduates are as likely to be unemployed as high school graduates (**Table 5.5**). In all three surveys, about 60 percent of respondents think that university graduates are as likely as a high school graduate to be unemployed, while only one-third disagree. There is majority agreement in nearly all social groups, including those with different levels of schooling and in most occupational classes; even the university educated are roughly split. The only clear dissent is from corporate executives, two-thirds of whom reject this statement. In fact, the executive perception is correct; high school graduates have remained about twice as likely as university graduates to be unemployed throughout the past decade.[86] But the public consensus reflects a widespread sense of a scarcity of suitable jobs for young people in general as well as concern about high unemployment in general.

In light of this consensus, in the current survey we have probed further to assess the extent to which the public think that higher

TABLE 5.6
'Over the next five years there won't be enough jobs to go around no matter how much training and education people get.'

	%
Agree	55
Disagree	33
Neither/not stated	12

N=1000

education is actually associated with individuals' getting better jobs when they do get them (**Table 5.5**). An overwhelming majority – over 80 percent – agree that university graduates are more likely to obtain a better job with higher income than a high school graduate. The consensus is general across all social categories. In spite of popular perceptions of substantial unemployment and underemployment of university graduates, public recognition of the occupational value of formal schooling seems very strong.

Future Job Prospects

So how hopeful are people about the future availability of jobs in relation to educational attainments? According to the responses summarized in **Table 5.6**, a majority (55 percent) of Ontarians now think that there won't be enough jobs to go around over the next five years, regardless of how much additional training and education people get; only one-third disagree. Women are more likely to be pessimistic (60 percent) than men (50 percent). Clear majorities in most employee classes express negative expectations, while corporate executives and small employers are more likely to be optimistic. These findings are generally consistent with those of the *Maclean's* 1996 year-end poll concerning the reduced economic expectations of Canadians.[87]

Policies

In this section we examine public preferences regarding a range of policy options that could affect future relations between education and work: workfare versus training, support for research and development, and low-wage or reduced-workweek strategies for job creation.

TABLE 5.7
'Should programs designed to get people off welfare and back to work stress ...'

	%
Community public works jobs at minimum wage	24
Short-term training for low-skilled jobs	22
Longer term training for higher skilled jobs	39
Combinations	7
Can't say	8

N=1000

Workfare versus Training

In an effort to get people off the public welfare rolls and back into employment, the present Ontario government has introduced a program to provide public-works jobs identified by community organizations to welfare recipients at a minimum wage. Such 'workfare' programs have been experimented with previously in other places with mixed results.[88] The question reported in **Table 5.7** gauges how much public support there is for a workfare strategy in comparison with alternative training strategies for getting welfare recipients back into the active workforce.

Only about one-quarter of Ontarians express relative support for workfare, while most prefer training. A plurality of about 40 percent would like to rely on longer-term training for higher-skilled jobs to help get welfare recipients back to work; short-term training for low-skilled jobs is about as popular as workfare. Even when public works and short-term training are combined, there is less than majority support (46 percent) for these 'low wage' strategies. The only significant social-group differences are by occupational class, with majorities of service and industrial workers and the unemployed – the groups that tend to be most vulnerable to becoming welfare recipients – being the most likely to favour longer-term training strategies.

Canadian Research and Development

It has been widely documented that Canada has been spending less in per capita terms on research and development than most other OECD countries for many years.[89] This fact applies to both public and private research spending. There has been plenty of recent media

80 Public Attitudes towards Education in Ontario 1996

TABLE 5.8
'Presently Canada spends less on research and development than most other industrialized countries. In general, do you think Canada should spend more, not change the amount spent, or spend less on research and development?'

	%
Spend more	69
Spend same amount	22
Spend less	4
Can't say	5

N=1000

argument both bemoaning Canada as a branch plant economy and celebrating the benefits of drawing on the research innovations of our trading partners, notably the United States. Current views of Ontarians on what should be done with research spending are summarized in **Table 5.8**.

More than two-thirds of Ontarians now would like to see more spent on Canadian research and development; less than one-quarter would prefer to maintain current levels, while less than 5 percent want further reduction. This consensus extends across nearly all social groupings. The only significant exception is by level of schooling; university-educated respondents are the most supportive (75 percent), but even a plurality of those with elementary schooling (45 percent) agree. These results, combined with the previous finding of majority support for university research funding, suggest substantial public sentiment in favour of concerted government research policies as a general development strategy.

Lower Wages or Shorter Workweeks?

The OECD Jobs Study of 1994 recommended lowering 'training wages' relative to average wages for job entrants in any occupation in order

TABLE 5.9
'The minimum wage for young people should be lowered if this would create more jobs for youth.'

	Agree %	Disagree %	Don't know %	N
1994	37	58	5	1070
1996	28	66	6	1000

TABLE 5.10
'Government should establish a shorter standard work week and restrict overtime so that employers will need to hire additional employees.'

	Agree %	Disagree %	Don't know %	N
All respondents	55	36	10	1000
Age				
18–24	40	40	20	133
25–34	50	42	8	236
35–44	58	35	8	208
45–54	60	36	4	143
55–64	62	36	2	118
65+	64	21	15	143
Sex				
Male	49	43	8	483
Female	61	29	10	517
Occupational class				
Corporate executives	17	75	9	114
Small employers	41	59	–	41
Self-employed	52	38	10	115
Managers	58	38	4	91
Professional employees	53	35	12	87
Supervisors	46	47	7	158
Service workers	55	33	12	109
Industrial workers	63	27	10	58
Homemakers	55	33	12	50
Unemployed	54	34	12	39
Retired	68	21	11	172
Students	45	46	9	50

to induce firms to provide more places.[90] We have assessed Ontarians' support for this type of strategy in the last two surveys. The results appear in **Table 5.9**.

This low-wage strategy was rejected by a clear majority (58 percent) in 1994, and opposition has increased to two-thirds this year; supporters have correspondingly decreased. The only notable difference is on occupational class. In fact, only corporate executives remain plurality supporters; all other occupational classes are now firmly opposed, including over three-quarters of those in the groups likely to be most directly affected – students and industrial workers.

At the end of 1994, the federal government released the report of the Advisory Group on Working Time and the Distribution of Work, which endorsed a new public priority emphasizing redistribution and reduction of working time.[91] The present survey asks for views on reduced standard workweeks as a means to create more jobs for others (**Table 5.10**).

There is now majority support (55 percent) for reduced workweeks to create more jobs; over one-third disagree, and 10 percent are uncertain. There are important differences by age, sex, and occupational class. Older people and women are somewhat more likely to agree. The largest differences are by occupational class. Clear majorities of small employers and especially corporate executives oppose this strategy, while majorities in most employee categories, particularly industrial workers, favour it. The expressed support among professional-managerial employees and unionized industrial workers is quite interesting, because research studies have found that employees remaining in these groups are actually most likely to have been working longer and longer hours during the past generation, while other workers have increasingly been relegated to involuntary part-time employment or unemployment.[92] Public policy initiatives along the lines of the federal Advisory Group's proposals may now represent the most politically popular means of employing unused skills and of generally improving education–job relations.

6
Further Education, Computers, and Libraries

This chapter is about issues in adult education. The first section looks at patterns of participation, including both formal courses and self-directed, informal learning activities. The second and third sections are concerned with two major resources for further education and the relationship between them: computerized information networks and public libraries.

The first section, on personal participation in further education, includes:

- patterns of participation in formal courses over the past decade
- types of courses taken and credits earned
- reasons for taking courses
- hours of work-related and general-interest, informal learning per week

The second section deals with personal contact with computers and views on computerized information networks, including:

- access to a personal computer at home and at work
- ability to use a personal computer for basic tasks
- general impact of computerized information networks on people
- responsibility of government to guarantee affordable access to computerized networks

The final section looks at the role of libraries, beginning with their relationship to computerized information networks. Issues include:

TABLE 6.1
'Have taken a continuing education course in the past year.'

	1986 %	1988 %	1990 %	1992 %	1994 %	1996 %
All respondents	20	24	31	36	27	28
Age						
18–24	24	38	43	53	25	38
25–34	25	33	43	47	40	37
35–44	28	32	35	41	35	33
45–54	17	16	25	34	24	34
55–64	10	11	15	19	19	16
65+	6	6	13	8	9	3
Schooling						
Elementary	3	5	5	15	8	5
High school incomplete	10	16	27	26	17	16
High school complete	14	23	26	25	21	20
Community college	31	35	37	45	33	37
University	31	36	43	44	36	36
	N=1042	N=1011	N=1032	N=1000	N=1070	N=1000

- role of libraries in providing access to the Internet
- role of libraries in providing access to on-line government services
- importance of libraries and other cultural institutions for adult education
- importance of libraries for particular categories of adult learners

Adult and Continuing Education

Participation in adult and continuing education courses is similar to the rate found in the 1994 survey (see **Table 6.1**). During the period from 1986 to 1992, participation had increased in each survey, but in 1994 the rate declined by about one-third from 36 percent to 27 percent. In 1996 the rate remained approximately the same as 1994, at 28 percent.

There is now little variation by age category except for the lower participation of respondents in the oldest two categories. Prior schooling remains highly correlated with participation in adult and continuing education courses, with higher rates for those who have community college and university backgrounds. Participation rates in 1996 are similar among all occupational classes in the active labour force.

TABLE 6.2
'Where did you take these courses?'

	1994 %	1996 %
Community college	36	44
University	15	27
High school	13	11
Offered by your employer	10	4
Private school or college	7	11
Community organization or agency	6	4
Correspondence	5	4
Offered by your professional association	4	3
Other	9	7
	N=294	N=284

Note: Percentages total slightly more than 100 because some respondents selected more than one option, indicating multiple courses.

As **Table 6.2** indicates, most adult and continuing education courses are taken at public institutions. The community college remains the primary location for most adult or continuing education. In fact, there has been a significant increase in the number of courses taken at postsecondary institutions (community college and university) in 1996, with stable patterns in other categories.

TABLE 6.3
'Did any of the courses provide credit for a diploma, certificate or degree?'

	1994 %	1996 %
Type of credit		
Community college	31	32
University	15	24
High school	12	12
No credit indicated	51	44
	N=294	N=284

Note: Percentages total slightly more than 100 because some respondents selected more than one option, indicating multiple credits.

In both 1994 and 1996, most respondents report taking courses for credit (see **Table 6.3**). About one-third of all courses result in credit from a community college, while a further one-quarter earn university credit. About one in ten respondents reports earning a high school

TABLE 6.4
'Which one of the following best captures your main reason for taking adult education courses?'

	1994 %	1996 %
To help me do my present job better	35	36
To prepare me for a new job	21	21
Out of general interest	21	19
To obtain a diploma, certificate or degree	15	12
To meet other practical needs unconnected with work	7	12
Can't say	1	1
	N=294	N=284

credit. The growing number of courses taken at university, as reported above, has produced parallel increase in university course credits.

The main reasons given for taking adult and continuing education courses are similar in 1996 to those given in 1994 (see **Table 6.4**). The most prevalent reason is 'to help me do my present job better' followed by 'to prepare me for a new job' and 'out of general interest.' Fifty-seven percent of respondents indicate that their main motivation was job-related. If we assume that courses taken to secure a degree, diploma, or certificate might also be related ultimately to employment prospects, then 69 percent of the courses were taken for work-related reasons.

Table 6.5 indicates who paid fees or tuition for courses taken, by age, prior schooling, and occupational class. (Some respondents cited more than one source.) As in past OISE/UT surveys, most adult or continuing education courses are paid for by the individual. In 1996, we find a notable increase in the proportion of individuals who paid for a course themselves, while most other categories (family, employer, government, union, other) remain fairly constant. There is

TABLE 6.5
Source of fee payment, by age, prior schooling, and occupational class.

	Self %	Family %	Empl. %	Gov. %	Union %	Other %	N
All participants							
1994	60	3	24	13	2	6	294
1996	70	3	21	14	<1	6	284

Note: Multiple responses were accepted, and so totals may exceed 100%.

TABLE 6.6
'Did your employer, a government agency or some other organization require or recommend any of the courses you took in the past year?'

	1994 %	1996 %
Required	6	11
Recommended	17	13
Neither	77	76
	N=294	N=284

no significant decline in the proportion who report that employers paid fees.

Participating in adult and continuing education remains primarily a voluntary activity, with three-quarters of all courses in both 1994 and 1996 being neither recommended nor required by employers or government (see **Table 6.6**). There may be a small increase in courses reported to be required, but the overall pattern remains the same.

In 1996 we asked respondents about the amount of time that they spend in informal learning – namely, work-related or undertaken out of general interest – outside the context of courses. (The full wordings of the questions are provided in **Table 6.7**). Respondents were directed to include under 'work-related' any learning (outside of courses) related to 'paid or household work, or work you do as a volunteer.' **Table 6.7** shows the average number of weekly hours of work-related learning, learning for general interest, and total weekly hours of learning activity for all respondents. Work-related learning averages 5.7 hours a week (or 5.9, if we include only those currently employed); the average for general-interest learning is 6.2 hours. The average for all informal learning is 11.6 hours a week.

In the case of informal activities, we do not see the same relationships to age and prior schooling as we see for courses (see **Table 6.1**). Taken together these two tables may mean that almost everybody participates in informal learning, while taking courses is highly constrained by institutional requirements and policies.

Computers: Access and Impact

We are now in a transitional period – access to information and opportunities to pursue formal and informal learning are becoming increasingly computer-based. Access to computer networks and the

88 Public Attitudes towards Education in Ontario 1996

TABLE 6.7
'Please think of any learning you do on your own or with others that is *not* part of organized schooling or continuing education courses. This includes *any* activities in which your main purpose is to gain specific knowledge or skills.'

'Not counting coursework, about how many hours in a typical week do you spend trying to learn anything *related to your paid or household work, or work you do as a volunteer.* Just give your best guess.'

'Not counting coursework about how many hours in a typical week do you spend trying to learn *anything of general interest* to you? Just give your best guess.'

	Work-related (average hours/week)	General interest (average hours/week)	General interest and work-related* (average hours/week)	N
All respondents	5.7	6.2	11.6	935†
Age				
18–24	7.1	6.7	13.7	122
25–34	6.6	5.8	12.0	220
35–44	5.7	6.0	11.4	201
45–54	4.8	5.2	9.7	138
55–64	5.8	6.9	12.0	107
65+	3.4	7.1	10.1	130
Schooling				
Elementary	5.4	8.6	13.2	35
High school incomplete	5.4	6.4	11.5	107
High school complete	5.9	6.9	12.5	235
Community college	6.2	5.8	11.6	197
University	5.5	5.7	10.8	346

* Includes learning for general interest and work-related learning.
† Excludes those who did not respond to *either* question. Note that 890 offered an estimate of time spent in work-related learning and 922 offered an estimate for general-interest learning. (This includes those who stated that they spent no time in either or both types of learning activity.)

facility to use them are not yet essential. However, this is clearly a major trend, and those who have access to networks and the skills to use them are already gaining advantages over those on the outside.[93] It is not uncommon now, as an example, for government reports to be publicly accessible on the Internet before 'hard copies' are readily available. This was the case for the Report of the Advisory Panel on Future Directions for Postsecondary Education. New developments in distance education are oriented to computer-mediated learning. Reductions in opening hours and staffing in public libraries confer an

TABLE 6.8
'Do you have access to a personal computer at home, at work or both?'

	%
No access	31
At home only	18
At work only	15
Both	36
Not stated	<1

N=1000

advantage to those who can use computerized catalogues unassisted from their own home or workplace computers.

Personal Access and Computer Skills

The growing importance of basic computer literacy and of the ability to get access to and use computerized networks has sparked concerns about the breadth and equity of network access and acquisition of computer skills. In 1996 we asked for the first time whether respondents had access to a computer at home, at work, or both. About one-third report no access to a personal computer (see **Table 6.8**). Of those with access, about one-half have a personal computer available either at home or at work, while the remainder have access at both sites.

Tables 6.9 and **6.10** look at patterns of access separately for work and home. Among those employed at the time of the survey, 70 percent had access to a personal computer on the job. Access varied with the educational requirement set by employers for the positions held by respondents and by type of occupation. Only one-half of those in jobs where there was no set educational requirement reported access, compared to over 90 percent of those holding positions requiring a university degree. The overwhelming majority of executives, managers, small employers, and the self-employed indicated having access, compared to barely one-half of service workers and less than one-third of industrial workers.

There are also significant differences in access to computers at home. Overall, 54 percent of respondents indicated having access. Women (49 percent) are less likely than men (58 percent) to report availability. Less than one-third of respondents fifty-five and over, compared to a majority of all other age groups, have home access. There are

TABLE 6.9
Access to a computer at work by education required for job and occupation

	%	N
All employed respondents	70	666
Education required		
No specific requirement	50	99
High school diploma	60	182
Community college certificate	77	107
University degree	91	211
Occupational class		
Corporate executives	89	114
Small employers	78	41
Self-employed	66	115
Managers	98	91
Supervisors	74	158
Professional employees	78	87
Service workers	57	109
Industrial workers	29	58

also differences by educational attainment. Less than one-third of those without a high school diploma, about 40 percent of diploma holders, but a majority of respondents with postsecondary education report a home computer. Finally, as shown in **Table 6.10**, respondents reporting family incomes of $80,000 or more are about twice as likely to have such access as those from families with incomes under $40,000.

TABLE 6.10
Home access to a computer by family income

	%	N
All respondents	54	1000
Family income		
Under $20,000	39	87
$20,000–$29,999	29	127
$30,000–$39,999	37	109
$40,000–$59,999	57	169
$60,000–$79,999	70	132
$80,000+	76	161

In 1996 we again asked respondents about whether they could use a personal computer for tasks such as word-processing and electronic

TABLE 6.11
'Can you do things like word processing or sending electronic mail on a computer?'

	Yes %	No %	Not stated %	N
All respondents				
1994*	60	40	<1	1070
1996	62	37	<1	1000
Age				
18–24	81	18	0	133
25–34	72	27	1	236
35–44	69	31	1	208
45–54	74	26	0	143
55–64	48	52	0	118
65+	19	81	0	143
Schooling				
Elementary	9	91	0	40
High school incomplete	32	68	0	121
High school complete	48	51	1	249
Community college	66	34	0	207
University	85	15	<1	366

* In 1994, the question was: 'Can you do anything besides play games on a computer, for example, do word processing or send electronic mail?'

mail. The results are essentially unchanged from 1994; about 60 percent have at least the basic computer skills cited in the question (see Table 6.11). This is similar to the national figure of 56 percent obtained by the Statistics Canada General Social Survey in 1994.[94] Age and education continue to be powerful predictors of whether individuals have basic computer skills, as shown in **Table 6.11**.

Impact of Computerized Networks

The 1996 OISE/UT survey included a series of questions on computerized information networks. We initiated this series to gather baseline data on public perceptions and views on policy. While use of networks, notably the Internet, is growing rapidly, a fact of which the media remind us almost daily, only a small minority, about 10 percent of households, currently use networks.[95]

As **Table 6.12** indicates, 70 percent of the public think that computerized information networks will benefit people's lives. This view is

TABLE 6.12
'Do you think that the general effect of new computerized information networks on peoples lives will be positive, negative or make little difference?'

	%
Positive	70
Negative	12
Make little difference	13
Can't say	6

N=1000

general across social groups, including a bare majority among those over sixty-five.

Both Statistics Canada and industry studies estimate that only 10 percent of households have access to computer networks such as the Internet. To the constraints of equipment (and equipment costs) can be added the expense of subscribing to a service providing Internet access. How to make computerized networks generally accessible, particularly by the disadvantaged, has become a major policy issue. The fact that governments seek to offer information and services on-line has given the question added importance.

Is access to the Internet sufficiently important for government to guarantee access at affordable cost to most Ontario residents? In 1996, two-thirds of respondents think that the government has a responsibility in this area (see **Table 6.13**). This view is general across social groups, especially among the young and those in the lowest income groups. Over 80 percent of respondents under twenty-five support guaranteed access, compared to 47 percent of those sixty-five and older (the only age group where less than one-half were supportive.) There is a similar range in the case of income, but a majority in all income groups favour guaranteed, affordable access. Among corporate executives, however, a large majority (71 percent) disagree.

TABLE 6.13
'Do you think that government should be responsible for making sure that there is a place where people can connect to computer networks like the Internet, at a cost most people can afford?'

	%
Yes	67
No	27
Can't say	6

N=1000

Roles for Libraries

Access to Networks

A benchmark in the growth of computerized information networks has been the transformation of public, institutional (for example, university), and private libraries. Computerized library catalogues available both locally and over the Internet, computerized search facilities, and computerized information holdings have changed libraries very significantly over the past decade. In some jurisdictions, public libraries are seeking a central role in providing public access to computerized information networks. This would include remote access to the computerized catalogues of the libraries themselves, access to on-line services offered by all levels of government, and, most broadly, access to the Internet. The Alberta government is establishing an electronic library network linked to the Internet. In Ontario, a similar initiative is being explored under the title Network 2000.[96]

The case for public libraries' becoming the main public access point for those not willing or able to use commercial services rests on their traditional role in providing universal, affordable access to information, including government documents, and the expertise that they have acquired in adapting their own organizations to computerized information networks. There are, however, other public and private organizations with interests and expertise in this area.

The 1996 OISE/UT survey included three questions on the role of libraries. The first two dealt with the relative competence of public libraries compared to other organizations (schools, community agencies, private businesses) to provide access to and instruction in the use of the Internet and access to and assistance in using government services on-line. The third question asked whether or not public libraries should become the main place for public access to computerized information networks for those unable to connect with them from home or work.

As **Table 6.14** indicates, almost three-quarters of respondents think that public libraries would be better at providing access to computer networks and instructions on how to use them than other organizations. A smaller majority hold the same view regarding access and assistance in using government services on-line. Views are similar across social groups, including corporate executives. An overwhelming majority support making libraries the main point of public access for

TABLE 6.14
'For people who cannot connect to computer networks at their home or office, public access might be provided by organizations such as public libraries, schools, community agencies or private business. Do you think public libraries would be better, about the same, or worse at each of the following:'

	Better %	About the same %	Worse %	Can't say %	N
Providing access to computer networks like the Internet, along with instructions on how to use them	74	14	6	6	1000
Providing connections and assistance in using government services over a computer network, for example, applying for a permit	56	25	10	9	1000

computerized networks (see **Table 6.15**). Again this view is general across social groups.

Support for public libraries as access points may rest on two different but complementary foundations. First, their role does not seriously challenge commercial services used from home or the workplace. Second as units in a highly visible, generally trusted, and ubiquitous network of local, information-based institutions, libraries have virtually no obvious rival among public bodies for the role. (The school system is handicapped by a mandate focused on youth rather than the general population.)

Importance for Adult Learners

The 1996 survey also included a set of questions on the importance of the public libraries for the learning activities of adults. The current

TABLE 6.15
'Do you think public libraries should become the main place where people can use computerized information networks in local communities if they cannot connect from their home or workplace?'

	%
Yes	81
No	14
Can't say	4

N=100

TABLE 6.16
'How important do you think each of the following are in furthering the education of adults after completing their formal schooling?'

	Very important %	Somewhat important* %	Not very/not at all important %	Can't say %	N
Public libraries					
1990	54	38	8	0	1032
1996	77	21	1	<1	1000
Educational TV					
1990	24	49	26	1	1032
1996	41	48	9	2	1000
Science centres					
1990	19	51	29	1	1032
1996	32	52	15	2	1000
Museums					
1990	6	40	54	0	1032
1996	22	46	30	2	1000

* In 1990, 'fairly important.'

survey repeated a shortened version of a question originally asked in 1990, dealing with the role of different cultural institutions in adult continuing education. A second question asked about the role of public libraries for particular categories of adult learners.

Table 6.16 compares public ratings of the importance of four cultural institutions in 1996 with responses to a similar question asked in the eighth OISE/UT survey in 1990. The questions asked in each year differ slightly in terms of scale ('fairly important' in 1990 versus 'somewhat important' in 1996) and institutions presented (the 1990 list included educational radio, historic sites, theatres, and art galleries). Two main patterns are evident in the table. First, there has been a systematic re-evaluation of cultural institutions in the further education of adults who have completed their formal schooling. The proportion of respondents who rated each institution as very important to adult education is significantly greater in 1996 than in 1990. Second, there is a consistent ordering of institutions in each year according to their contribution to adult education. Public libraries head the list in each year and represent the only institution (of eight in 1990, four in 1996) rated very important by a majority. Educational TV, science centres, and museums follow. Views on the importance of cultural institutions to adult learners are similar across social groups.

96 Public Attitudes towards Education in Ontario 1996

TABLE 6.17
'How important do you think public libraries are for providing information to each of the following?'

	Very important %	Somewhat important %	Not very/ not at all important %	Can't say %	N
Adults taking educational courses or training programs	60	34	4	2	1000
Adults engaged in learning activities on their own	65	30	3	1	1000
Adults looking for information on local education and training programs	46	40	10	4	1000
Adults looking for marketing and financial information to run small businesses	43	40	11	6	1000

Building on this result, **Table 6.17** compares public perceptions of the importance of public libraries for different categories of adult learners. The public makes little distinction in the value of libraries to those taking formal training as compared to those engaged in learning on their own. In both instances a majority rate libraries as very important. Ratings for more specific purposes – getting information on local educational training programs and obtaining information connected with running a small business – are somewhat lower, on average, dividing about evenly between very and somewhat important. Views are again similar across social groups.

In October 1996 the provincial government announced legislation to allow public libraries to charge user fees for some basic services – a contentious issue – including the possibility of an annual membership fee, a practice adopted in several Alberta cities.[97] Current legislation allows charges for special services only, such as room rentals and photocopying. The purpose of the legislation is to allow municipalities to raise funds locally in the face of announced reductions in provincial support for libraries. Our 1996 survey asked respondents whether they support or oppose allowing an annual membership fee. Almost two-thirds say that they would support an annual fee (see **Table 6.18**). This view is general across social groups. Younger respondents are less supportive, but even among those under twenty-five a majority would

TABLE 6.18
'Do you support or oppose allowing public libraries to charge an annual membership fee for use of the library?'

	Support %	Oppose %	Can't say %	N
All respondents	62	33	5	1000
Age				
18–24	52	47	1	133
25–34	56	40	4	236
35–44	62	31	8	208
45–54	70	28	2	143
55–64	67	32	1	118
65 +	71	19	10	143

accept them. Somewhat surprisingly, views are similar across income groups, suggesting that respondents with low incomes anticipate only a modest annual charge.

Appendix: Methods

The Main Sample

Sampling Procedures and Representativeness

The 1996 OISE/UT survey involved a representative random sample of 1,000 adult Canadian citizens, eighteen years of age and over, who were interviewed by telephone in their residences across Ontario between September 30 and November 3, 1996. The survey was administered by the Institute for Social Research at York University. Respondents entered the survey through a two-stage sampling procedure. Random digit-dialling procedures were used to produce a sample of phone numbers. (In this procedure, phone numbers are computer-generated rather than relying on telephone directories, which exclude unlisted numbers.) Non-residential numbers were eliminated as ineligible when contacted. Within the households contacted, the adult resident was selected who was next to have a birthday. Ten or more call-backs were made in 15 percent of cases in attempts to reach respondents. A response rate of 63 percent was obtained.

As in previous OISE/UT surveys, the 1996 sample has been weighted to remedy slight imbalances in age and gender groups as indicated in **Table A1**. The weighted sample continues to somewhat underrepresent those with less than high school completion, and overrepresent those with postsecondary education. Thus, for example, while 41 percent of the weighted sample report no postsecondary education, this is the case for 53 percent of the adult Ontario population, based on 1991 census results.

TABLE A1
Age and gender weights

	Males	Females
18–24	1.366	1.242
25–34	1.043	0.926
35–44	0.767	0.745
45–54	1.087	0.747
55–64	1.185	1.587
65+	1.280	1.224

Changes in Methods from Prior Surveys

This is the second year in which the OISE/UT survey has been conducted by telephone rather than through personal interviews at home. The sampling procedures are just as valid in generating a representative sample of Ontarians as those used in surveys prior to 1994. In Ontario, over 98 percent of homes have telephones.[98] The demographic profile of respondents to our survey closely matches that for the 1992 survey. (A demographic breakdown of the weighted sample is provided in **Table A2**.)

The move to telephone rather than personal interviews should have had little influence on how people respond. It could be a problem where highly sensitive questions are asked – for example, about personal use of illegal drugs. It is reasonable to assume that respondents may be more willing to admit to illicit drug use over the telephone than in a face-to-face interview. This was, in fact, the dilemma faced by the Addiction Research Foundation (ARF) survey of drug use when it made the change from personal to telephone interviewing. While we were considering the change to a telephone survey, ARF generously made available to us the results of its internal analyses of the effects of changing interview methods. These showed no significant influence of interview method for almost all measures.[99] Our own questions, of course, are very much less sensitive. However, questions that we might consider for a face-to-face interview, where respondents can be given a written version of the item, are not practical over the telephone. This restriction has not prevented us from extending trend lines on most past questions.

Categories of Background Variables

Some clarification of the categories employed for occupational class, contact with schools and region may be helpful.

TABLE A2
Demographic breakdown of the sample

	%	N
Age		
18–24	13	133
25–34	24	236
35–44	21	208
45–54	14	143
55–64	12	118
65+	14	143
Unclassified	2	18
Sex		
Male	48	483
Female	52	517
Contact with schools		
Child at private elementary/high school	1	10
Child at Catholic elementary/high school	7	72
Child at public elementary/high school	19	193
Child at postsecondary only	6	58
Student	5	50
No formal contact	61	605
Education		
Elementary	4	40
High school incomplete	12	121
High school complete	25	249
Non-university postsecondary	21	207
University	37	366
Unclassified	2	18
Religion		
Protestant	48	479
Catholic	32	318
Jewish	1	12
Other	3	25
No religion	15	146
Unclassified	2	19
Mother tongue		
English	77	772
French	6	57
Other European	12	124
Non-European	4	42
Unclassified	1	5
Ethnic group		
British	50	503
French	8	76
Other European	24	242

TABLE A2 (continued)

	%	N
Non-European	11	105
Unclassified	7	74
Family income		
Under $20,000	9	87
$20,000–$29,999	13	127
$30,000–$39,999	11	109
$40,000–$59,999	17	169
$60,000–$79,999	13	132
$80,000+	16	161
Unclassified	21	214
Occupational class		
Corporate executives	–	114
Small employers	4	41
Self-employed	12	115
Managers	9	91
Professional employees	9	87
Supervisors	16	158
Service workers	11	109
Industrial workers	6	58
Homemakers	5	50*
Unemployed	4	39
Retired	17	172*
Student	5	50*
Unclassified	3	31
Region		
Metro Toronto	31	175
Metro outskirts	18	287
Eastern Ontario	13	174
Western Ontario	23	242
Northern Ontario	14	122
Total	100†	1070

* Categories are not fully consistent with those used in 1992 (see 'Categories of Background Variables').
† Percentages may not add to 100 for all variables because of rounding.

Occupational Class

With the exception of the sample of corporate executives (outlined below), we base the categorization of occupational class for those in the labour force initially on an aggregation of 'unit groups' of occupations as listed in the Standard Occupational Classification Manual – Statistics Canada, *Standard Occupational Classification 1980*

(Ottawa: Statistics Canada, Feb. 1981). One key modification made is the separate categorization of those owning their own business or self-employed under the headings 'small employers' or 'self-employed.' Small employers are defined as those owning their own business and having (fewer than fifty) paid employees. The self-employed category is restricted essentially to those working for themselves alone or in partnership. The classification used since 1990 differs somewhat from previous years in terms of how the division between managers and supervisors is drawn and in the definition of industrial versus service workers. (Details are available from the authors.) The category of student includes those who identify their main occupation as student or their main source of income as student assistance.

Contact with Schools

The 'contact with schools' variable has been substantially revised since 1992. We now focus on three groups: those who have children in elementary and/or secondary school (whether or not respondents themselves are taking courses), those who do not have children in school but are taking courses themselves, and those who have no contact with educational institutions, either directly or through their children. **Table A2**, however, provides a more detailed breakdown.

Region

Our division of the province into geographical regions is now based on telephone exchanges. The Metro Toronto region is defined as area code 416. Metro outskirts is area code 905; western Ontario, 519; eastern Ontario, 613; and northern Ontario, 705 and 807. The main difference between these divisions and those used in earlier surveys is that 'Metro outskirts' now includes the Niagara peninsula, which was categorized as western Ontario prior to 1994.

The Supplementary Sample of Corporate Executives

A special survey of corporate executives has been conducted in each year of the survey, as individuals in this small but influential occupational class would be unlikely to appear in sufficient numbers within the main population sample. We have drawn the sample from all the corporate directors resident in Ontario and engaged in managing corporations based in the province, as listed in the Financial

104 Appendix

TABLE A3
Recommended allowance for sampling error of a percentage

Sample size	1000	600	400	200	100
Percentages near					
10	2	4	4	5	7
20	3	4	5	7	9
30	4	5	6	8	10
40	4	5	6	9	11
50	4	5	6	9	11
60	4	5	6	9	11
70	4	5	6	8	10
80	3	4	5	7	9
90	2	4	4	5	7

Post *Directory of Directors*, 1996. From this group we took a sample of 347 by simple random selection.

The special survey was conducted using a mail questionnaire – the only affordable method. We received 114 usable responses and nineteen returns to sender, due to out-of-date addresses or changes in employment. Subtracting the latter from the original sample size, we find that our response rate is 32 percent.

Sampling Tolerances

In this study, we take the opinions and preferences of 1,070 respondents to represent those of all adult residents in Ontario. In the case of findings for subgroups, the numbers are smaller – 517 women represent all women in the province, 366 respondents with university stand in for all those over eighteen years of age with this level of schooling. (These are in fact the weighted totals.) For any sample survey, there will usually be differences between the findings for these relatively small numbers of representatives and the results that would have been obtained if the entire population had been surveyed.

Table A3 provides estimates of error for any percentage taken by itself. The estimate indicates that the actual percentage for the population might be the stated number of percentage points either greater or less than the percentage actually shown in the table. For example, in **Table 1.1** (see page 15), 34 percent of all respondents in 1996 indicated that they were dissatisfied with the Ontario school system. The estimate of the possible sampling error for this statistic is found in **Table A3** at the intersection of the row for 'percentages

Methods 105

near 30' and the column for sample size of 1,000 (since the percentage is based on the entire sample of 1,000).

The estimate of sampling error is ±percent – that is, if the survey had covered the entire population of Ontario, chances are 95 in 100 that the percentage satisfied with the school system in general would have fallen between 30 percent and 38 percent.

The error estimates in this table are based on the assumption of simple random sampling (SRS). While the OISE/UT survey departs SRS because adults in smaller households generally have more chance of being selected than those in larger households (since most homes will have only one phone for adults), the estimates in **Table A3** should provide generally reliable guides for estimates of sampling error for OISE/UT survey findings. The effect of our departure from SRS is that the sample size is equivalent to a somewhat smaller simple random sample. Readers should thus make conservative judgments in using particular columns of Table A3.

Sampling error must also be taken into account for the differences between percentages for different groups. Again the error estimates become larger, the smaller the groups involved. Differences among groups reported in the text have passed this test.

Notes

1 As quoted in W. Walker, 'School Reform To Be Massive Snobolen Says,' *Toronto Star*, May 28, 1996, p. A9, *Business Plan: Ontario Ministry of Education and Training* (Toronto: Queen's Printer for Ontario, May 1996).
2 Letter from chairs of the seventeen public school boards in the Greater Toronto Area to the minister of education, as quoted in P. Small, 'Boards Seek Talks with Snobolen,' *Toronto Star*, November 17, 1996, p. A5.
3 Jurgen Habermas, 'The Public Sphere: An Encyclopedia Article (1964),' *New German Critique* 1 (Fall, 1974), p. 50.
4 Royal Commission on Learning, *For the Love of Learning: Report of the Royal Commission on Learning* (Toronto: Queen's Printer for Ontario, 1994).
5 For a brief overview, see A. Duffy, 'School Reform a Campaign No-show,' *Toronto Star*, May 30, 1995, p. A19.
6 See, for example, A. Duffy, 'Education Report into the "Vapour,"' *Toronto Star*, January 28, 1996, p. A2; L. Wright, 'Core Math, English Studies to Be Slashed,' *Toronto Star*, April 24, 1996, p. A3.
7 See H. Levy, 'Crowds at Queen's Park Protest Education Cuts,' *Toronto Star*, January 14, 1996, p. A14; V. Dwyer, 'Class Warfare,' *Maclean's*, February 12, 1996, pp. 72–4; D. Barry, 'Thousands Turn out at Ministry of Education,' *Varsity*, October 28, 1996, p. 1.
8 W. Walker, 'School Report on New Funding Fails to Impress,' *Toronto Star*, June 11, 1996, p. A8; P. Small, 'School-Funding to be Studied by Panel,' *Toronto Star*, September 12, 1996, p. A33; D. Girard, 'School Tax Overhaul Planned,' *Toronto Star*, September 20, 1996, p. A1; B DeMara, 'Business Tax Pool Urged for Education,' *Toronto Star*, December 31, 1996, p. A1.
9 Advisory Panel on Future Directions for Postsecondary Education, *Excellence, Accessibility: Report of the Advisory Panel on Future Directions for Postsecondary Education* (Toronto: Queen's Printer for Ontario, 1996).

10 This commissioned report was written by Windsor lawyer Leon Paroian. See P. Small, 'After-school Work Part of job?" *Toronto Star*, November 2, 1996, p. A28.
11 S. McCarthy, 'Private Religious Schools Lose Funding Court Case,' *Toronto Star*, November 22, 1996, pp. A1, 33; D. Vienneau, 'Church out of Nfld. Schools,' *Toronto Star*, December 5, 1996, p. A15.
12 Quoted in D. Girard, 'Bigger Cuts to Schools in Future: Snobolen,' *Toronto Star*, September 19, 1996, p. A3.
13 For insightful recent discussions of the formation of democratic consent and of the stages in this process, see T. Glasser and C. Salmon, eds., *Public Opinion and the Communication of Consent* (New York: Guilford Press, 1995).
14 For a thought-provoking account of the historical development of the concept of public opinion, and of the democratizing and refeudalizing tendencies of public opinion polls, see J. Peters, 'Historical Tensions in the Concept of Public Opinion,' in T. Glasser and C. Salmon, eds., *Public Opinion and the Communication of Consent*, pp. 3–32. Mass media accounts of education have often been misleading and unresponsive to general public interest, as documented by G. Kaplan, *Images of Education: The Mass Media's Version of America's Schools* (Washington, D.C.: Institute for Educational Leadership, 1992); and S. Elam, *How America Views Its Schools* (Bloomington, Ind.: Phi Delta Kappa, 1995).

Both corporations and governments frequently conduct opinion polls which they are reluctant to release to the general public. For example, the Ontario government has recently been accused by teachers' federations and others of producing a 'push poll' to support its cost cutting education plans. The poll in question, conducted in early February 1996 and publicly released in compliance with a freedom of information request, does contain several unbalanced questions with a limited range of options, leading respondents to support further cutbacks in education spending. See Bradgate Research Group, *Ontario Province Wide Survey of Educational Issues* (Toronto: Ministry of Education and Training, February 1996).
15 R. Lerner, A. Nagai, and S. Rothman, 'Elite vs. Mass Opinion: Another Look at a Classic Relationship,' *International Journal of Public Opinion Research* 3 no. 1 (Spring 1991), 1–31.
16 On deliberative polling, see J. Fishkin, *The Voice of the People: Public Opinion and Democracy* (New Haven, Conn.: Yale University Press, 1995); on referenda and other means of direct democratic decision making, see 'A Survey of Democracy,' *Economist*, 341, 7997 (December 21, 1996), 74.1–14.

17 An extensive, 1994 survey funded by both government and private-sector organizations found widespread general hostility to current government performance and that 86 percent of Canadians wanted government to consult citizens more. See Ekos Research Associates, *Rethinking Government* (Ottawa: Ekos, 1995); and E. Greenspon, 'Maintain Services, Canadians Tell Survey,' *Globe and Mail*, February 25, 1995, pp. A1, 6.

18 The ten prior surveys have all been published in Toronto as *Public Attitudes toward Education in Ontario* by OISE Press. Authors and years of surveys are as follows: D.W. Livingstone (1978); Livingstone and D. Hart. (1979 and 1980); Livingstone, Hart, and L.D. McLean (1982); Livingstone, Hart, and L.E. Davie (1984, 1986, 1988, 1990, 1992, and, 1994).

19 The most recent major, publicly available, Canada-wide education poll is T. Williams and H. Millinoff, *Canada's Schools: Report Card for the, 1990s* (Toronto: Canadian Educational Association, 1990). Comparable regular education opinion polls have been published in the United States since the late, 1960s (see S. Elam, L. Rose and A. Gallup, 'The 28th Annual Gallup Poll of Attitudes toward the Public Schools,' *Phi Delta Kappan* 78 no. 1 [1996] pp. 41–59), and in the United Kingdom since, 1983, as part of a general social-opinion survey (see R. Jowell, L. Brook and L. Dowds, eds., *International Social Attitudes: The 10th BSA Report* [Aldershot: Dartmouth Publishing Company, 1993]). For a comparative analysis of the OISE, American Gallup and other foreign opinion surveys on educational issues, see N. McEwen, 'Public Perceptions: Implications for Educational Reform,' (paper presented at the annual meeting of the American Educational Research Association, New York, April 9, 1996).

20 We were able to test this hypothesis in, 1990. The eighth OISE survey administered in 1990, was followed in spring 1991 by an Institute for Social Research (ISR) poll which asked: 'In general, how satisfied are you with the education system in Ontario? Would you say you are ... very satisfied, somewhat satisfied, somewhat dissatisfied, or very dissatisfied,' While there are several differences in question wordings, it seem reasonable to assume that the lack of a middle term in the ISR question would be the most consequential in producing any differences from the OISE survey result. The ISR poll found that 62 percent were satisfied, compared to a figure of 50 percent for the 1990 OISE Survey where, 19 percent of respondents had indicated that they were neither satisfied nor dissatisfied.

In the current year we were able to compare OISE survey results with those of the February 1996 survey by Bradgate Research Group sponsored by the Ministry of Education and Training, which again asked about satisfaction using a question without a middle option ('How satisfied are you with the education system?'). The ministry's survey also recorded a somewhat higher proportion of satisfied respondents than did the OISE survey – 57 percent versus 50 percent.

21 See S. Elam and L. Rose, 'The 28th Phi Delta Kappan/Gallup Poll of the Public's Attitudes toward the Public Schools,' *Phi Delta Kappan*, 78 no. 1 (1996), p.45.
22 Ontario Ministry of Education and Training, *Excellence in Education: High School Reform, A Discussion Paper* (Toronto: Queen's Printer of Ontario, 1996).
23 Children currently in high school will in most cases not be affected; the four-year program will begin after they have graduated. We do not know, however, how many parents of current high school students were aware of this.
24 See A. Duffy, 'Most Teachers Frustrated by Destreaming, Poll Finds.' *Toronto Star*, February 28, 1995, pp. A1–2.
25 See S. Elam, L. Rose, and A. Gallup, 'The 27th Annual Gallup Poll of Attitudes toward the Public Schools,' *Phi Delta Kappan*. 77 no. 1 (1995), p.47. In the U.S. Gallup poll this question was preceded by one that asked whether raising standards would encourage or discourage students from low-income backgrounds. Almost two-thirds of respondents indicated that they thought that 'students from poor backgrounds' would be encouraged by higher standards.
26 In 1994 and in 1984 in Ontario, about one-third thought that quality had deteriorated over the previous five years, while just over 40 percent saw no change in quality or an improvement. While this question was not asked in 1996, it seems unlikely that there has been any marked change in public views, given their long term stability. In 1994 we identified at worst a slight erosion over the period 1988–94 in the proportion of respondents who saw improvement. See Livingstone, Hart and Davie, *Public Attitudes* (1994), pp. 22–3.
27 See ibid., pp. 23–4.
28 Peter Small, 'Parents Call for Provincial "Exit Exam."' *Toronto Star*, December 1, 1996, p. A3.
29 *Final Report of the Ontario School Board Reduction Task Force* (Toronto: Publications Ontario, [February] 1996).
30 See P. Small, 'After-School Work Part of Job?' *Toronto Star*, November 2, 1996, p. A28.
31 See Livingstone, Hart, and Davie, *Public Attitudes* (1994), n21.

32 Ontario Parent Council, *Report on the Establishment of School Parent Councils in Ontario* (Toronto: Ontario Parent Council, July 15, 1994).
33 Royal Commission on Learning, *For the Love of Learning*, pp.48–51, 75–6
34 See Livingstone, Hart and Davie, *Public Attitudes* (1994) p.16.
35 See Alberta Education, *Roles and Responsibilities in Education: A Position Paper* (Edmonton: Alberta Education, December 1994). This document defines the role of school councils, in part, as follows (pp.17–18): 'The school council's role is to work with and provide advice to the school principal and sometimes to the school board. Their involvement may go beyond fund-raising activities and special events ... The school council can, at its own discretion, be involved in: • deciding what type of programs to offer, where options are available (with the principal, teachers, parents and students) • deciding what extracurricular activities the school will offer (with the principal, teachers, parents and student council) • determining standards of student conduct and discipline (with the principal, teachers, parents and students).'
36 See S. Kastner 'New Era in N.B.; Schools without Trustees.' *Toronto Star*, September 28, 1996, p. A1.
37 See Richard Brennan, 'Ban Teachers' Strikes: Report,' *Toronto Star*, November 1, 1996, p. A9.
38 See Livingstone, Hart, and Davie, *Public Attitudes* (1994) pp.18–19.
39 Royal Commission on Learning, *For the Love of Learning*, p. 78.
40 See A. Duffy, 'Blacks, Gays School Plan to Go Ahead,' *Toronto Star*, August 23, 1995, p. A7; 'Worthy Initiative, Sneaky Method,' editorial, *Toronto Star*, August 29, 1995, p. A16; K. Casteneda, 'All-Girl Ideal Leaves Boys in Cold.' *Toronto Star*, April 24, 1996.
41 See R. Rees, *Women and Men in Education* (Toronto: Canadian Educational Association, 1990); 'More Women Heading up Elementary Schools: Report.' *Toronto Star*, August 14, 1996, p. A16.
42 See Peter Small, 'Male Teachers Vote to Join Women in New Federation "with Clout,"' *Toronto Star*, August 14, 1996, p. A16; Peter Small, 'Teachers' New Union Ends Sexual Segregation.' *Toronto Star*, August 15, 1996, p. A10.
43 Patrick Abtan , 'A 4th "R" that Schools Could Do without,' *Toronto Star*, July 16, 1996, p. A21.
44 D. Flavelle, 'School Bus Ads to Start Rolling in January,' *Toronto Star*, October 31, 1996, p. A3.
45 See, for example, 'Canadians Back Cuts, Poll Says,' *Toronto Star*, April 26, 1993, p. A11.
46 Greenspon, 'Maintain services.'

47 See Livingstone, Hart, and Davie, *Public Attitudes* (1990), pp. 6–7.
48 E. Greenspon, 'Seven Ways They'd Rather Go.' *Globe and Mail*. February 27, 1995, pp. A1, 5.; Ekos Research Associates, *Canadians' Spending Priorities* (Ottawa: Department of Finance, 1996).
49 A. Wilson-Smith, 'Future Imperfect: Canadians Are Ready for Fundamental Changes in Society.' *Maclean's*, 109 no. 53 (December 30, 1996/January 6, 1997), pp. 16–21. According to this survey, only 3 percent of Ontarians now see education as the most important issue facing Canadians, compared to 31 percent choosing unemployment, 11 percent government deficits, 8 percent national unity, 7 percent health care, and 6 percent other social services (p. 18).
50 W. Walker, 'Ontarians Think Services Poorer, Poll Reveals.' *Toronto Star*, April 27, 1996, p. A9; California Public Education Partnership, *What Californians Want from the Public Schools* (San Francisco: Center for the Future of Teaching and Learning, 1996), pp. 6–7; Elam and Rose 'The 28th Phi Delta Kappan/Gallup Poll,' p. 52.
51 For example, a Canadian Gallup poll conducted in August 1994 found majority support for increased funding of elementary, high school, and postsecondary education and that these levels of support had been essentially stable since, 1986. See Gallup Canada, *Majority Favour Increased Education Funding*, Gallup Poll, September 1, 1994. A December 1992 Angus Reid survey found that clear majorities in all provinces perceived universities to be underfunded by government and that this view was somewhat more common in most other provinces than in Ontario. See Angus Reid Group, *Assessments of Post-Secondary Education: Funding and Accessibility Issues* (Ottawa: Association of Universities and Colleges of Canada, January 8, 1993).
52 A continuing British survey of social attitudes cited in the *Economist* on November 19, 1994, p. 67, found that 87 percent of respondents wanted more government spending on health services and 79 percent favoured more education spending. A September 1994 MORI poll cited in the *Economist* on October 1, 1994, p. 72, found that 68 percent of British voters supported increasing income tax to pay for greater spending on education. Data from 1989 and 1993 surveys in New Zealand indicate that support for increasing government spending and taxes for the education system grew from 78 percent to 89 percent during this period, as reported in P. Perry and A. Webster, 'Value Changes from 1989 to 1993 in New Zealand: A Research Note,' (unpublished paper, Massey University, April 1994), p. 2.
53 See the sources cited in note 52.

54 The main recommendation was number 159: 'That equal per-pupil funding across the province, as well as additional money needed by some school boards for true equity, be decided at the provincial level, and that the province ensure that funds be properly allocated.' Royal Commission on Learning, *For the Love of Learning*. p. 79.
55 See Commission on the Financing of Elementary and Secondary Education in Ontario, *Report of the Commission on the Financing of Elementary and Secondary Education in Ontario* (Toronto: Ministry of Education, 1985); and Ontario Fair Tax Commission, *Fair Taxation in a Changing World* (Toronto: University of Toronto Press, 1993).
56 The more recent provincial bodies include the task force headed by Anne Golden on the Greater Toronto Area, which reported in January 1996 and the 'Who Does What' Committee, headed by David Crombie, which reported its relevant recommendations at the end of December 1996. See B. DeMara, 'Business Tax Pool Urged for Education.' *Toronto Star*, December 31, 1996, pp. A1, 26.
57 Livingstone, Hart, and Davie, *Public Attitudes* (1990), p. 7; R. James, 'Local Tax System Revamp Supported, Survey Finds.' *Toronto Star*, April 29, 1996, pp. A1, 6.
58 Working Group on Education Finance Reform, *Report to the Minister* (Toronto: Ministry of Education and Training, June, 1996). For reactions to this report, see W. Walker, 'School Report on New Funding Fails to Impress.' *Toronto Star*, June 11, 1996, p. A8.
59 P. Small, 'School-funding Taxes to Be Studied by Panel,' *Toronto Star*, September 12, 1996, p. A33; D. Girard, 'School Tax Overhaul Planned.' *Toronto Star*, September 20, 1996, pp. A1, 4.
60 A January 1994 Environics poll also found the Ontario public highly divided on this issue. See A. Duffy, 'Ontarians Split on School Taxes.' *Toronto Star*, January 23, 1994, p. A4.
61 McCarthy, 'Private Religious Schools.'
62 See Vienneau, 'Church out of Nfld. Schools,' and the series of background articles by Lois Sweet in mid-September, especially 'Provincial Funding for Religious Schools.' *Toronto Star*, September 15, 1996, p. F4.
63 S. Contenta, 'Overhaul Schools, Quebec Report Says,' *Toronto Star*, October 11, 1996, p. A11.1.
64 See Livingstone, Hart, and Davie, *Public Attitudes* (1988), pp. 10–11.
65 See V. Galt, 'Innovative Approaches to Education.' *Globe and Mail*, September 7, 1996, p. A5.
66 Elam and Rose, '28th Phi Delta Kappan/Gallup Poll,' p. 53.

67 A.M. Gallup, 'The 17th Annual Gallup Poll of the Public's Attitudes toward the Public Schools,' *Phi Delta Kappan*, 67 no. 1 (1985), pp. 46–7.
68 Advisory Panel, *Excellence, Accessibility*, p. 56.
69 Ibid., p. 13.
70 This type of question format is not uncommon in public opinion surveys where an issue is both complex and as yet little debated in public forums. It allows us to obtain both an initial reaction on the basic issue and indications as to how respondents would probably react as public debate unfolds. Nevertheless, the format has been much abused in so-called 'push polls,' where wording and order of questions are used to try to shape responses in a particular direction.
71 The *Maclean's* 1996 year-end poll asked respondents how likely they thought it was that by the year 2005, 'There will be private universities for those who are prepared to pay the full tuition fee.' Eighty percent thought that this was likely. Respondents were then asked how acceptable this was to them. Sixty-one percent indicated that private, full-fee universities were acceptable. Men were more acquiescent than women (69 versus 53 percent). Those in the 18–24 age group were more accepting (68 percent) than older respondents. See *Maclean's* 109, no. 53 (December 30, 1996/January 6, 1997), pp. 24, 46.
72 Judging from the results of a focus group sponsored by the Council of Ontario Universities, it seems likely that negative reaction to the qualification regarding fees reflects concerns about equality of access.
73 See Livingstone, Hart, and Davie, *Public Attitudes* (1992), chap. 7; Livingstone, Hart, and Davie, *Public Attitudes* (1994), chap. 7.
74 P. Small, 'Tuition Rates Soaring as Funding Cut: Report,' *Toronto Star*, August 20, 1996, p. A2.
75 Statistics Canada, 'Consumer Price Index – September 1996,' *Daily* (available on the Internet).
76 See, for example, T. Morganthau and S. Nayyar, 'Those Scary College Costs,' *Newsweek*, April 29, 1996, pp. 52–68.
77 Advisory Panel, *Excellence, Accessibility*, p. 3.
78 Ibid., particularly recommendations 6 and 7.
79 P. Small. 'University Grads Carry Fast-Rising Debt Loads,' *Toronto Star*, October 3, 1996, p. A15.
80 Advisory Panel, *Excellence, Accessibility*, p. 5.
81 For contrasting analyses, see D.W. Livingstone, *The Education–Jobs Gap: Underemployment or Economic Democracy* (Boulder, Col.: Westview Press, 1997); and L. Resnick and J. Witt, eds., *Linking School and Work: Roles for Standards and Assessment* (San Francisco: Jossey-Bass, 1996).

Notes to pages 73–100   115

82 Livingstone, Hart, and Davie, *Public Attitudes* (1994) p. 27.
83 The most influential early critical study was I. Berg, *Education and Jobs: The Great Training Robbery* (New York: Praeger, 1970).
84 See especially V. Burris, 'The Social and Political Consequences of Overeducation,' *American Sociological Review* 48 (August 1983), pp. 454–67.
85 See Livingstone, Hart, and Davie, *Public Attitudes* (1990) p.18.
86 See Statistics Canada, *The Labour Force*, monthly, Cat. No. 71-001.
87 J. Chidley, 'Reduced Expectations,' *Maclean's*, 109, no. 53 (December 30, 1996/January 6, 1997): pp. 22–5.
88 Adil Sayeed, 'Workfare: An Overview of the Issues,' *Policy Options*, 16 no. 4 (May 1995), pp. 3–5.
89 Organization for Economic Co-operation and Development (OECD), *Main Science and Technology Indicators, 1996*, 1 (Paris: OECD, 1996).
90 OECD, *The OECD Jobs Study: Facts, Analysis, Strategies* (Paris: OECD, 1994), p. 48.
91 Advisory Group on Working Time and the Distribution of Work, *Report of the Advisory Group* (Ottawa: Minister of Supply and Services, December 1994), pp. 52–3.
92 See J. Schor, *The Overworked American* (New York: Basic Books, 1991); and A. Yalnizyan, 'Securing Society: Creating Canadian Social Policy,' in A. Yalnizyan, T.R. Ide, and A. Cordell, *Shifting Time: Social Policy and the Future of Work* (Toronto: Between the Lines, 1994), pp. 17-71.
93 For an overview of empirical data on the increasing importance of computer literacy and computer access, see J. Oderkirk, 'Computer Literacy – a Growing Requirement.' *Educational Quarterly Review* 3 no. 3 (1996), Statistics Canada Cat. No. 81-003-XPB.
94 See Oderkirk, 'Computer Literacy,' p. 3.
95 Jim Bronskill, 'Canadian Internet Users to Top 1 Million,' *Toronto Star*, January 3, 1997, p. E3.
96 See Ontario Ministry of Citizenship, Culture and Recreation (MCCR), *Network 2000: Creating Ontario's Virtual Library* (Toronto: MCCR, October 1996).
97 Canadian Press, 'Ontario to Pave Way for Fees at Libraries.' *Toronto Star*, October 19, 1996, p. A3. On the contentious nature of user fees, see, for example, 'Preserve Libraries,' editorial, *Toronto Star*, December 16, 1996, p. A4.
98 Statistics Canada, *Household Facilities and Equipment Catalogue* (Cat. No. 64-202), 1992.
99 The exception was cocaine use, where the telephone survey yielded a significantly higher figure than personal interviews. See Edward M. Adlaf

and Donna Mates, *A Comparison of Telephone and Personal Interview Surveys for Estimating Alcohol and Other Drug Use* (unpublished, Addiction Research foundation [ARF], Toronto, 1993).